Kaliviḍambanam –
With Explanations

*

*Kamalātmānandatha*ḥ @ **Dr. Ramamurthy N.**

M.Sc., B.G.L., CCCP, DSADP, CISA, PMP, CGBL, Ph.D.

*

*

Name: *Kaliviḍambanam* – With Explanatio[n]

First Edition: 2025

Author: *Kamalātmānanda Nāthaḥ* [
Dr. Ramamurthy N,
http://ramamurthy.jaagru[/]

ISBN (13):   978-93-341-9[5]

978-93-34195682

Number of pages:

Price: ₹ [...]

Printed at:

Published by:

*****

Table of Contents

*****

Dedication

Apāra Karuṇa Sindhum Jnānadam Śāntha Rūpiṇam ।

Śrī Candraśekhara Gurum Pranamāmi Mudānvaham ॥

अपारकरुणा सिन्धुम् आनदम्शान्तरूपिणम् ।

श्रीचन्द्रशेखर गुरुम् प्रणमामि मुदान्वहम् ॥

This book is humbly dedicated to all human beings in Kali Yuga, who follow their dharma as much as possible and avoid sinful activities. May Lord Kali bestow his blessings to all.

Kamalātmānanda Nāthaḥ @ Dr. Ramamurthy N

*****

16/04//2025

The great scholar Sri Neelakanda Deekshidar, who was born in the lineage of Appaiya Deekshidar, was a devout devotee of Goddess Meenakshi.

Neelakanda Deekshidar, who was a minister of King Tirumala Nayaka in Madurai, eventually attained Vairagyam and accepted Sanyasa. He stayed in a village called Palamadai in Tirunelveli and attained enlightenment there on the Shukla Paksha Ashtami day of the Dhanur month (December-January). Every year, the worship of that great man is celebrated at his adhisthanam there.

His works are numerous! Although there are devotional books like Shiva Leelarnavam and Ananda Sagarastavam, the humorous book Kali Vidambanam is a text that many scholars enjoy and celebrate.

Kali Vidambanam means laughing at Kali and it is a small work with 102 songs. This book criticises the evils of the Kali Yuga. On the other hand, Deekshith's commentary is a false praise.

We live in this Kali Yuga, which is the last in the order of Kruta, Treta, Dwapara and Kali Yugas. In Kali Yuga, Dharma will be very low, people will be selfish, morality and virtue will decrease, Material and lustful desires will prevail and natural disasters.

This book, which describes all these evils of the Kali Yuga, details each piece of information directly and humorously. This book, written in Samskrutam, is composed of very simple words. It consists of short poems.

In Kali Vidambanam, it satirically points out many things such as the problems caused by caste and religious differences, fake scholars, doctors, sorcerers, and many contradictions in society.

It is worth noting that even though it was written in the 16th century C.E., the contents are still very much relevant today.

Our disciple Dr. Ramamurthy has compiled it, with a beautiful Tamil/English explanation, we can easily understand the meaning, even if we do not know Samskrutam,

Many such rare hidden things should be brought to the knowledge of common people. Our congratulations to Dr. Ramamurthy, who is doing this noble work!

We sincerely bless him, his family and all the readers of this book to live forever with the perfect grace of Sri Bhuvaneshwari Devi.

Bliss   Propitious   Auspicious

Jaya Bhuvaneshwari

ஸ்ரீ ப்ரணவாநந்த ஸ்வாமின:
Sri Bhuvaneswari Avadhoota Vidhya Peetam
Pudukkottai

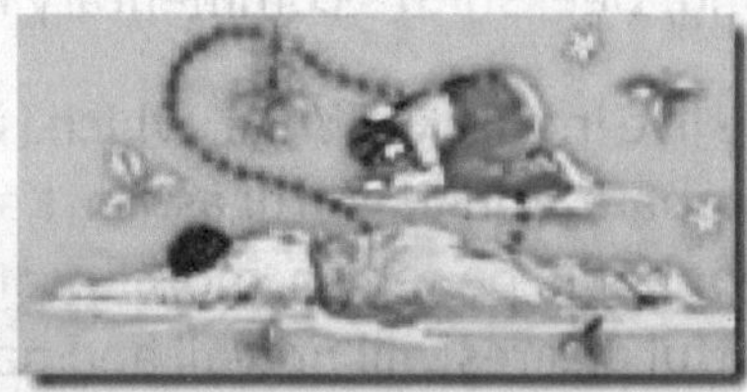

*****

Introduction

Oṃ Śrī Gurubhyo Namaḥ | ॐ श्री गुरुभ्यो नम: |

Let us delve about some aspects of various yugas and the time periods as per Hindu mythology. This will enable us to more clearly comprehend the purpose and context of this Stotram.

A Yuga Cycle (also called as Chatur yuga, or Maha yuga, etc.) is a cyclic age. Each cycle lasts for 4,320,000 years (12,000 divine years) and repeats four yugas (world ages) – *Kruta* or *Satya Yuga*, *Treta Yuga*, *Dvapara Yuga* and *Kali Yuga*.

As a Yuga Cycle progresses through the four yugas, each yuga's length and humanity's general moral and physical state within each yuga decrease by one-fourth. Kali Yuga, which lasts for 432,000 years, is believed to have started in 3,102 B.C.E. Near the end of Kali Yuga, when virtues are at their worst, a cataclysm and a re-establishment of *dharma* will occur to usher in the next cycle's Kruta (Satya) Yuga, prophesied to occur by Kalki.

There are 71 Yuga Cycles in a Manvantara (age of Manu) and 1,000 Yuga Cycles in a Kalpa (day of Brahma).

A cyclic age encompassing the four yuga ages are defined in three texts – Surya Siddhanta, Manusmruti and Shrimad Bhagavata Purana.

A cyclic age of the divine, celestial, or Devas encompass the four yuga ages. The texts give a length of 12,000 divine years, where a divine year lasts for 360 solar (human) years. A cyclic age encompassing the four yuga ages.

It is theorised that the concept of the four yugas originated sometime after the compilation of the four Vedas, but prior to the rest of the other texts, based on the concept's absence in the former writings.

It is believed that the four yugas—Kruta (Satya), Treta, Dvapara and Kali—are named after throws of an Indian game of long dice, marked with 4-3-2-1 respectively. A dice game is described in the Rig Veda, Atharva Veda, Upanishats, Ramayana, Mahabharata and other Puranas, while the four yugas are described after the four Vedas with no mention of a correlation to dice.

A complete description of the four yugas and their characteristics are detailed in the Vishnu Smriti (chapter 20), Mahabharata (Vanaparva 149, 183), Manusmruti (81–86) and Puranas (Brahma, chapter 122–123; Matsya, chapter 142–143. The four yugas are also described in the Bhagavata Purana (3.11.18–20).

Duration and structure – texts describe four yugas in a Yuga Cycle—Kruta (Satya) Yuga, Treta Yuga, Dvapara Yuga and Kali Yuga — starting in order from the first age, each yuga's length decreases by one-fourth (25%), giving proportions of 4:3:2:1. Each yuga is described as having a main period (viz. yuga proper) preceded by its yuga-sandhyā (dawn) and followed by its yuga-sandhyāṃśa (dusk), where each twilight (dawn/ dusk) lasts for one-tenth (10%) of its main period. Lengths are given in divine years (years of the gods), each lasting for 360 solar (human) years.

Each Yuga Cycle lasts for 4,320,000 years (12,000 divine years) with its four yugas: Kruta (Satya) Yuga for 1,728,000 (4,800 divine) years, Treta Yuga for 1,296,000 (3,600 divine) years, Dvapara Yuga for 864,000 (2,400 divine) years and Kali Yuga for 432,000 (1,200 divine) years.

Structure of a yuga cycle

Yuga	Part	Divine years	Solar years
Kruta (Satya)	Sandhya (dawn)	400	144,000
	Proper	4,000	1,440,000
	Sandhyamsa (dusk)	400	144,000
Treta	Sandhya (dawn)	300	108,000
	Proper	3,000	1,080,000
	Sandhyamsa (dusk)	300	108,000

Yuga	Part	Divine years	Solar years
Dvapara	Sandhya (dawn)	200	72,000
	Proper	2,000	720,000
	Sandhyamsa (dusk)	200	72,000
Kali	Sandhya (dawn)	100	36,000
	Proper	1,000	360,000
	Sandhyamsa (dusk)	100	36,000
	Total	12,000	4,320,000

The current cycle's four yugas have the following dates based on Kali Yuga, the fourth and present age, starting in 3,102 B.C.E. and supposed to end 428,899 C.E.

We are currently in the;

- Second half of Brahma's life (Maha-Kalpa). 51st year of 100 (2nd half or Parardha)
- 1st month of 12
- 1st Kalpa (Shveta-Varaha Kalpa) of 30
- 7th manvantara (Vaivasvata Manu) of 14
- 28th Chatur-yuga of 71
- 4th yuga (Kali Yuga) of 4

Yuga dates are used in sankalpa, which is read out at the beginning of any rites to specify the elapsed time in Brahma's life.

With this background let us try to understand the Stotram on hand with more introduction.

Writing meanings and comments for Samskruta verses is not an easy task. The meaning and beauty of the source should not be fragmented but the clarity of the words should captivate the mind of the readers. The readers should dissolve and melt in the mind of the author of the source. The comments should be written in such a way that the readers can enjoy the sweet juice in it.

Conventions – The transliterated Samskrutam or other language words are written in *italics*. When Samskruta words are transliterated in English diacritical marks are used for proper pronunciation like;

ā – as in *Rama* *ḍ* – as in mu<u>d</u>
ḍh – as in go<u>dh</u>ood *ḥ* – visarga in as in *Rāmaḥ*
ī – as in p<u>ee</u>l *ṇ* – as in pu<u>n</u>
ṛ – as in st<u>r</u>ewn *ś* – as in <u>Sh</u>ankar
ṣ – as in fi<u>sh</u> *ṭ* – as in cu<u>t</u>
ṭh – as in an<u>th</u>ill *ū* – as in r<u>oo</u>t

Humble pranams to HH *ŚrīŚrī* **Prnavānanda Swāmijee**, who has blessed me and the readers with his nice introduction and some pleasantries. He only gave me an order with love to write this book. I am glad that I could fulfill his orders. Also, I am fortunate to have association with people like **Swāmijees**, who are my *Gurus*. Sincere thanks are due to all who helped me in bringing this book so nicely.

Appreciation and acknowledgements are due to all those who supported in this noble cause. The readers are requested to feel free in providing feedback. Let all the readers be blessed with glory of Gods.

This book is also being written by the same author in Tamil simultaneously.

Om Tat Sat

Chennai
2025 **Dr. Ramamurthy N**

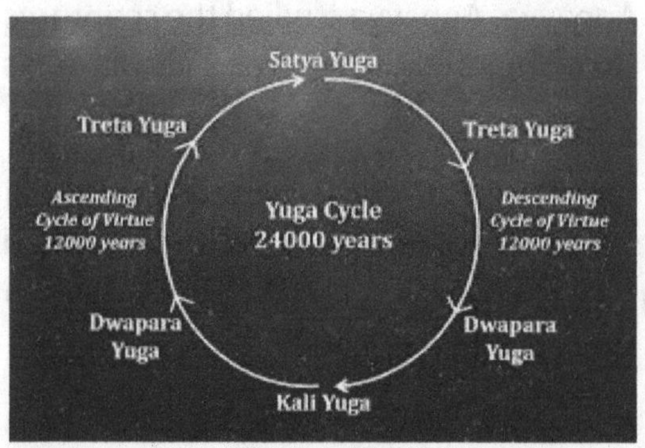

*****

Kaliviḍambanam

During the period of 16th and 17th centuries Samskruta scholars like Sri Appayya Dikshitar, Sri Neelakanta Dikshitar, Sri Govind Dikshitar, Sri Venkata Makkhi, Sri Rama Bhadra Dikshitar, Sri Yagya Narayan Dikshitar, Sri Raja choodamani and so on are very famous. Out of these Sri Neelakanta Dikshitar is like a lodestar.

<u>Appayya Dikshitar</u> – Appayya Dikshitar 1520–1593 C.E., was a performer of yajnas as well as an expositor and practitioner of the Advaita Vedanta philosophy but with a focus on Shiva or Shiva Advaita. After Sri Adi Shankara he was a prolific Advaita philosophy.

Appayya Dikshitar was born as Vinayaka Subramanian in Adaya-palam, near Arani in the Tiruvannamalai district, in Tamil Nadu, in the Krishna Paksha of the Kanya month of Pramateecha Varsha under the Uttara Proshtapada constellation of the Hindu calendar.

His father's name was Rangarajadhwari. Appaya, earlier had the name Vinayaka Subramanya. Acharya Dikshitar or Acchan Dikshitar was the younger brother of Appayya. Appayya studied the scriptures under his Guru, Rama Kavi. He completed the fourteen Vidyas at his young age itself.

Dikshitar had travelled widely, entering into philosophical disputations and controversies in many centers of learning. He had the rare good fortune of being revered and patronized in his own lifetime by kings of Vellore, Tanjore, Vijayanagara and Venkatagiri.

He was a well-learned in every branch of Samskrutam and has written many works, large and small. Our misfortune, only 60 of them are, however, extant now. These include works on Vedanta, Shiva Advaita, Meemamsa, Vyakarana, Kavya Vyakhyana, Alankara and devotional poems.

Dikshitar wrote the Chatur-mata-sara to illustrate the philosophical thoughts of the four prominent schools of interpretation of Brahma sutras. The Nyaya-Manjari deals with Advaita, the Naya-mani-mala with Srikanta mata, the Naya-mayukha-malika with Ramanuja's philosophy and the Naya-muktavali with Madhva's philosophy. He is said to be an incarnation of Lord Shiva and at the end united with Chidambaram Nataraja as Jyoti form.

Nīlakaṇṭha Dikshitar – Mahakavi Sri Neelakanta Dikshitar was born

near the end of the 16th century C.E., on 23rd May 1594, in the Tamil month of Vaikasi in the Jaya year of Tamil Panchangam. He is of the Bharadwaja Gotra and a Sama Vedi. He was an ardent devotee of Goddess Meenakshi. He was the grand-son of younger brother of Sri Appaya Dikshitar. Sri Neelakanta Dikshitar was the son of Shri Narayana Dikshitar and Bhoomi Devi Ammayar. He lost his parents and grandfather at a very young age and was brought up by Sri Appayya Dikshitar who was also his initial Guru. Later he studied under the guidance of Sri Venkata Makhi, Son of Famous Sri Govinda Dikshitar. Sri Venkata Makhi was a renowned musician. It was he, who codified the melakarta Ragas of Carnatic music.

Nīlakaṇṭha Dikshitar, was a minister at the Court of King Thirumalai Nayak Madurai, in the early 17th century C.E., was one of the most prolific poet-scholar of the age. Among Nīlakaṇṭha many literary oeuvres, is a delightful and amusing poem, Kaliviḍambana (A Mockery of the Kāli Age), that catalogues the fallen characters of the present age. A keen student of the contemporary society, Nīlakaṇṭha, at his wittiest best, pokes fun at people whose conduct he thinks is corrupt and questionable.

During his ministerial job in the royal court of Tirumalai Nayaka King of Madurai, under his supervision the Vasantha Mandapam or now known as Pudu Mandapa, at Madurai Meenakshi Amman Temple was built. He also dug Vandiyur Theppakulam a big Pond. During excavatory work for the Pond a Ganapati Idol was found and named as Mukkuruni Vinayagar placed now in Madurai Meenakshi Amman Temple. During his old age he settled at Palamadai Village in Tirunelveli District and place further south of Madurai. Palamadai village was actually gifted to him by Thirumalai Nayaka King.

Sri Neelakanta Dikshitar had authored several literary classics. Some of them are;

1. *Gaṅgāvataraṇam,*
2. *Vairāgyaśatakam,*
3. *Naḷacaritram,*
4. *Kaliviḍambanam,*
5. *Ānandasāgarastavaḥ,*
6. *Śāntivilāsaḥ,*
7. *Śivotkarṣamañjarī,*
8. *Mukundavilāsaḥ,*
9. *Raghuvīrastavaḥ,*
10. *Caṇḍīrahasyam,*
11. *Anyāpadeśaśatakam,*
12. *Nīlakaṇṭhavijayacampūḥ,*
13. *Kaiyaṭavyākhyānam,*
14. *Sabhārañjanaśatakam,*
15. *Gururājastavaḥ,*
16. *Śivatattvarahasyam* and
17. *Śivalīlārṇavaḥ.*

There is no clear evidence of the time period of Sri Appayya Dikshitar and Sri Neelakanta Dikshitar. Historical evidences suggest that the reign of king Tirumala Nayaka of Madurai was between 1623 and 1659 C.E. Since, he served in the court of Thirumalai Nayaka, it can say inferred that he must have lived during this period.

Though, it is not clearly known, it seems that this scholar and minister seemed to have adopted the Sannyasa Ashram, in his old age and spent his time in solitude and life of spiritual bliss, in a village by name Palamadai on the banks of river Thamirabarani in Tirunelveli District and attained Mukti in that village.

Kali Yug – At the fag end of Dvapara yuga, after the end of Kurukshetra battle, Ashwatthama tried to kill entire Pandava family including the baby in the womb of Uttara, wife of Abhimanya, son of Arjuna. But Lord Krishna protected the baby and he was the emperor Parikshit who ruled the Hastinapuram.

On account of the curse from a sage, Parikshit was about to die in 7 days through a snake bite. The snake by name, Dakshagan, who earlier had a revenge with Pandavas now ready to bite and kill Parikshit. Now that the death is confirmed, the king decided to spend the remaining 7 days fruitfully to attain Moksham. Sage Shuka

Brahmam explained Shrimad Bhagavatam in 7 days to the king and almost the entire upper world, other sages, everyone were present there. This is the practice followed even now to chant Bhagavata Saptaham (7 days). Naimisaranyam, in Uttar Pradesh is the place where this happened. Presently Bhagavata Saptaham is chant throughout 365 days by one or many groups.

There are 6 chapters called Bhagavata Mahatmyam (greatness of Bhagavatam) in Padma Puranam, Uttara Kandam. It clearly states Parikshit's rule was so Dharmic that Kali Purusha could not enter any of the house in his kingdom. Kali Purusha came to the emperor and asked him what is the way out. Parikshit told him you can enter the house where the people do not follow the prescribed dharma. That is the end of Dvapara yuga and start of Kali Yuga.

Shrimad Bhagavatam 12-2-1, details the Symptoms (characters) of Kali-yuga. It is mentioned here that in the Kali Yuga, Dharma Devata herself stands on one leg only. It clearly relates that, when the bad qualities of the age of Kali will increase to an intolerable level, the Supreme Personality of Godhead will descend as Kalki to destroy those who are fixed in irreligion. After that, a new yuga-cycle will begin.

As the age of Kali progresses, all good qualities of men diminish and all impure qualities increase. Atheistic systems of so-called religion will become predominant, replacing the codes of Vedic laws. The kings will become just like highway bandits, the people in general will become dedicated to low occupations and all the social classes will become just like low castes. All cows will become like goats, all spiritual hermitages will become like materialistic homes and family ties will extend no further than the immediate relationship of marriage.

Originally there were 40 *samskāras* to be performed to each child. Considering the vagaries of this era (*kali Yuga*), *Āpastambar* has reduced this to Fifteen. While performing *poojas* to different Gods like Ganesh, Subramania, Shiva and so on, it is a practice to do *Prāna Prathishta*, during which as a mark of 15 *samskāras*, we used to chant *pranava mantra 'Oṃ'* for 15 times. In practice, however, even these 15 samskaras are not properly and regularly performed by all.

This number also varies from family to family and from region to region.

A gist of some of the characters of Kali Yuga mentioned the Bhagavatam are;

- Religion, truthfulness, cleanliness, tolerance, mercy, duration of life, physical strength and memory will all diminish day by day because of the powerful influence of the Age of Kali.

- In Kali-yuga, wealth alone will be considered the sign of a man's good birth, proper behavior and fine qualities. And law and justice will be applied only on the basis of one's power.

- Men and women will live together merely because of superficial attraction and success in business will depend on deceit. Womanliness and manliness will be judged according to one's expertise in sex and a man will be known as a brahmana just by his wearing a thread.

- A person's spiritual position will be ascertained merely according to external symbols and on that same basis people will change from one spiritual order to the next. A person's propriety will be seriously questioned if he does not earn a good living. And one who is very clever at juggling words will be considered a learned scholar.

- A person will be judged unholy if he does not have money and hypocrisy will be accepted as virtue. Marriage will be arranged simply by verbal agreement and a person will think he is fit to appear in public if he has merely taken a bath.

- A sacred place will be taken to consist of no more than a reservoir of water located at a distance and beauty will be thought to depend on one's hairstyle. Filling the belly will become the goal of life and one who is audacious will be accepted as truthful. He who can maintain a family will be regarded as an expert man and the principles of religion will be observed only for the sake of reputation.

- As the earth thus becomes crowded with a corrupt population, whoever among any of the social classes shows himself to be the strongest will gain political power.

- Losing their wives and properties to such avaricious and merciless rulers, who will behave no better than ordinary thieves, the citizens will flee to the mountains and forests.
- Harassed by famine and excessive taxes, people will resort to eating leaves, roots, flesh, wild honey, fruits, flowers and seeds. Struck by drought, they will become completely ruined.
- The citizens will suffer greatly from cold, wind, heat, rain and snow. They will be further tormented by quarrels, hunger, thirst, disease and severe anxiety.
- The maximum duration of life for human beings in Kali-yuga will become fifty years.
- By the time the Age of Kali ends, the bodies of all creatures will be greatly reduced in size and the religious principles of followers of varnashrama will be ruined. The path of the Vedas will be completely forgotten in human society and so-called religion will be mostly atheistic. The kings will mostly be thieves, the occupations of men will be stealing, lying and needless violence and all the social classes will be reduced to the lowest level. Cows will be like goats; spiritual hermitages will be no different from mundane houses.
- Family ties will extend no further than the immediate bonds of marriage. Most plants and herbs will be tiny and all trees will appear like dwarf śamī trees. Clouds will be full of lightning, homes will be devoid of piety and all human beings will have become like asses.

It is so clear, how the qualities of Kaliyuga mentioned above in the Shrimad Bhagavata Purana are so perfectly applicable to the present era. The same has also been very clearly written in poems called *Kaliviḍambanam* by Sri Neelakanta Dikshitar in advance.

When the age of Kali has almost ended, the Supreme Personality of Godhead will incarnate. He will appear in the village Śambhala, in the home of the exalted Brāhmaṇa Viṣṇuyaśā and will take the name Kalki. He will mount His horse Devadatta and taking His sword in hand, will roam about the earth killing millions of bandits in the guise of kings. Then the signs of the next Satya-yuga will begin to appear. When the moon, sun and the planet Brhaspati enter simultaneously into one constellation and conjoin in the lunar mansion Puṣyā, Satya-yuga will begin. In the order of Satya, Tretā, Dvāpara and Kali, the cycle of four ages rotates in the society of living entities in this universe.

Kaliviḍambana Stotram – Kali = Kali Yug *Viḍambana* = Gaelic speech. Among Neelakandar's many literary works, Kalividambanam (Gaelic ode of Kali Yuga) is a cheerful and funny poem. It lists the fallen events of the present age. Neelakandar, a keen student of contemporary society, with his great humor, he pokes fun at people who he thinks are corrupt and questionable behavior. This hymn is said to be the first chapter of the Kamalalaya Mahatmya. Its uniqueness is best understood by comparing it with, say, the 'kalimahima' section of Subhashita-ratna-bhandagara, an anthology of subhashitas, or the 'kalidharma-vipaka' parts found in numerous puranas.

Kaliviḍambana – Literally translated as "A farce on the age of kali", this century of verses, along with his other works, are ample proof of the fact that *Nīlakaṇṭha Dīkṣita* is a satirist par excellence. In this work, which explores the evil effects of the present epoch, Kaliyuga, the poet makes debaters, teachers, physicians, astrologers, rich men, relatives, money-lenders, backbiters, hypocrites, misers and even poets, the butt of sarcasm, humor and irony. All the 102 verses in this poem employ the simple *śloka* on *anuṣṭubh* meter, aptly suited for making witty comments.

Though this text was written in the beginning of the 17th century C.E. itself, this Kalividambana Stotram is a work depicting present day (21st Century C.E.) society conditions. social satire, giving advice to people on leading a good life, good conduct, the importance of peace and dispersion, extra especially in the Kali Yug This is a parody of life in the dark age. He brings the pathetic standards to which the ideal human values can sink into a base. It is an excellent parody and various kinds of people like *Bandhavaḥ* – Relatives, *Uttamarṇāḥ* – Lender, *Dāridryam* – Poverty, *Dhaninah* – Rich People, *Piśunāḥ* – Lazy People, *Lobhinah* – Greedy, *Dhārmikāḥ* – Virtuous and *Durjanāḥ* – Wicked and so on will act and behave in the current age of Kali through these 102 verses. He has very beautiful and excellent fore thought and explained for the sake of money how people will compromise values.

The poet has exhibited his wide range of literary talents in delineating the story and describing various episodes with a touch of humour here and there. His command over prose comes out superbly in this work, which has been divided in to five chapters called *āśvāsas*.

This stotram is not only to explain the negative aspects/ calamities of Kali Yuga. It also advises that everyone should be cautious and live with dharma to avoid such disasters.

In other yugas one has to perform lots of pooja, yagas, etc., to reach the God. Japa should be done. Yagna and other pujas, will be very difficult to perform and will also cost money. To do Japa, one must have focused, single-mindedness without any other thinking.

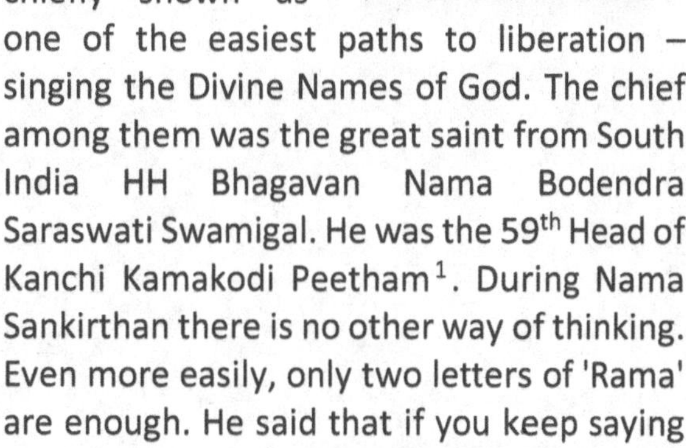

But in Kali Yuga, dedicated devotion is the best way to reach God. Srimad Bhagavatam says that devotion alone is enough. Prahlada describes nine-types of Bhakti (devotion). In this Kali Yuga, all the great saints, who have incarnated in this holy 'Bharata' have chiefly shown us one of the easiest paths to liberation – singing the Divine Names of God. The chief among them was the great saint from South India HH Bhagavan Nama Bodendra Saraswati Swamigal. He was the 59th Head of Kanchi Kamakodi Peetham[1]. During Nama Sankirthan there is no other way of thinking. Even more easily, only two letters of 'Rama' are enough. He said that if you keep saying the same thing over and over again, you can attain moksha. *'Ra ma'* are the two letters which converted Ratnakar into Valmiki. The letter *'Ra'* is the second letter in *'Narayana'* and the letter *'Ma'* is the second letter in *'Nama: shivaya'*. Hence, the word *'Rama'* is the combination of Vishnu and Shiva.

---

[1] Just for reference – PresentlyHH Vijayendra Saraswari Swamijee the 70th head, Kanchi Kamakoti Mutt,

Let us now try to comprehend and enjoy the Stotram verse by verse.

*****

Purāṇas – About Kali Yuga

Thousands of years ago, even before this Kalividambana Stotram was written, our other puranas and scriptures have predicted, how this Kali Yuga and how people will be in this Kali Yug. A preview about some of them.

The scriptures say that of the four yugas, Kaliyuga is the most dreadful one — it will give all difficulties. In this yuga, righteous activities will slow down and unrighteousness will be at its peak. Justice and dharma will be pushed back.

At the end of Dvapara yuga, all sages and saints were worried about the onset of Kaliyuga. They went to Sage Vedavyasa to enquire about how difficult it would be in this Kaliyuga. Reading their minds and predicting what they would ask, Vedavyasa himself gave a paradoxical reply — that it's very easy to attain salvation in Kaliyuga. The sages were dumbstruck with the reply, which went against much of what they had anticipated.

Kali Yuga, is the fourth, shortest and worst of the four yugas (world ages) in a Yuga cycle, preceded by Dvapara Yuga and followed by the next cycle's Kruta (Satya) Yuga. It is believed to be the present age, which is full of conflict and sin.

According to Puranic sources, Krishna's departing back to Vaikunta marked the end of Dvapara Yuga and the start of Kali Yuga, which is dated to 17/18 February 3102 B.C.E. Lasting for 432,000 years (1,200 divine years), Kali Yuga began 5,126 years ago and has 426,874 years left as of 2025 C.E. Kali Yuga will end in the year 428,899 C.E.

Near the end of Kali Yuga, when virtues are at their worst, a cataclysm and a re-establishment of dharma occur to usher in the next cycle's Kruta (Satya) Yuga, prophesied to occur by Kalki. A dialogue between Krishna and Ganga found in the Brahma Vaivarta Purana describes that for the first 10,000 years of Kali Yuga, the ill effects of Kali Yuga will be reduced due to the presence of bhakti yogis and the ability to nullify sinful reactions, after which Earth will be devoid of devout religious people and be shackled by Kali Yuga.

Gaudiya Vaishnavism believes this sub-period started later in Kali Yuga with the birth of Chaitanya Mahaprabhu (1,486 C.E.).

Shrimad Bhagavata Maha Purana the Twelfth Canto Chapter One;

The Degraded Dynasties of Kali-yuga

The Twelfth Canto of Shrimad Bhagavatam begins with Śrī Śukadeva Gosvāmī predicting the kings of the earth who will appear in the future during the Age of Kali. Then he gives a description of the numerous faults of the age, after which the presiding goddess of the earth sarcastically berates the foolish members of the kingly order who perpetually try to conquer her. Next Śukadeva Gosvāmī explains the four varieties of material annihilation and then he gives his final advice to Maharaja Parikshit. Thereafter King Parikshit is bitten by the snake Dakṣaka and leaves this world. Sūta Gosvāmī concludes his narration of Shrimad Bhagavatam to the sages at Naimiṣāraṇya forest by enumerating the teachers of the various branches of the Vedas and Puranas, relating the pious history of Markandeya Rishi, glorifying the Supreme Lord in His universal form and in His expansion as the Sun-God, summarizing the topics discussed in this literature and offering final benedictions and prayers.

The First Chapter of this canto briefly describes the future kings of the dynasty of Magadha and how they become degraded because of the influence of the Age of Kali. There will be twenty kings who ruled in the family of Pūru, in the dynasty of the sun-God, counting from Uparicara Vasu to Purañjaya. After Purañjaya, the lineage of this dynasty will become corrupted. Following Purañjaya there will be five kings known as the Pradyotanas, who are then followed by the Śiśunāgas, the Mauryas, the Śuṅgas, the Kāṇvas, thirty kings of the Andhra nation, seven Ābhīras, ten Gardabhīs, sixteen Kaṅkas, eight Yavanas, fourteen Turuṣkas, ten Guruṇḍas, eleven Maulas, five Kilakilā monarchs and thirteen Bāhlikas. After this, different regions will be ruled over at the same time by seven Andhra kings, seven Kauśalas, the kings of Vidūra and the Niṣadhas. Then the power of rulership in the countries of Magadha and so forth will fall to kings who are no better than fourth varnas and Milichas and are totally absorbed in irreligion.

Verses 1-2; Śukadeva Gosvāmī said; The last king mentioned in our previous enumeration of the future rulers of the Magadha dynasty was Purañjaya, who will take birth as the descendant of Bṛhadratha. Purañjaya's minister Śunaka will assassinate the king and install his own son, Pradyota, on the throne. The son of Pradyota will have Pālaka, his son will be Viśākhayūpa and his son will be Rājaka.

Verse 3; The son of Rājaka will be Nandivardhana and thus in the Pradyotana dynasty there will be five kings, who will enjoy the earth for 138 years.

Verse 4; Nandivardhana will have a son named Śiśunāga and his son will be known as Kākavarṇa. The son of Kākavarṇa will be Kṣemadharmā and the son of Kṣemadharmā will be Kṣetrajña.

Verse 5; The son of Kṣetrajña will be Vidhisāra and his son will be Ajātaśatru. Ajātaśatru will have a son named Darbhaka and his son will be Ajaya.

Verses 6-8; Ajaya will father a second Nandivardhana, whose son will be Mahānandi. O best of the Kurus! these ten kings of the Śiśunāga dynasty will rule the earth for a total of 360 years during the Age of Kali. My dear Parikshit, King Mahānandi will father a very powerful son in the womb of a fourth-class woman. He will be known as Nanda and will be the master of millions of soldiers and fabulous wealth. He will wreak havoc among the Kshatriyas and from that time onward virtually all kings will be irreligious fourth-class.

Verse 9; That lord of Mahāpadma, King Nanda, will rule over the entire earth just like a second Parashurama and no one will challenge his authority.

Verse 10; He will have eight sons, headed by Sumālya, who will control the earth as powerful kings for one hundred years.

Verse 11; A certain brahmin [Chanakya] will betray the trust of King Nanda and his eight sons and will destroy their dynasty. In their absence the Mauryas will rule the world as the Age of Kali continues.

Verse 12; This brahmin will enthrone Chandragupta, whose son will be named Vārisāra. The son of Vārisāra will be Aśokavardhana.

Verse 13; Aśokavardhana will be followed by Suyaśā, whose son will be Saṅgata. His son will be Śāliśūka, Śāliśūka's son will be Somaśarmā and Somaśarmā's son will be Śatadhanvā. His son will be known as Bṛhadratha.

Verse 14; O best of the Kurus! these ten Maurya kings will rule the earth for 137 years of the Kali-yuga.

Verses 15-17; My dear King Parikshit, Agnimitra will follow as king and then Sujyeṣṭha. Sujyeṣṭha will be followed by Vasumitra, Bhadraka and the son of Bhadraka, Pulinda. Then the son of Pulinda, named Ghoṣa, will rule, followed by Vajramitra, Bhāgavata and Devabhūti. In this way, O most eminent of the Kuru heroes, ten Śuṅga kings will rule over the earth for more than one hundred years. Then the earth will come under the subjugation of the kings of the Kāṇva dynasty, who will manifest very few good qualities.

Verse 18; Vasudeva, an intelligent minister coming from the Kāṇva family, will kill the last of the Śuṅga kings, a lusty debauchee named Devabhūti and assume rulership himself.

Verse 19; The son of Vasudeva will be Bhūmitra and his son will be Nārāyaṇa. These kings of the Kāṇva dynasty will rule the earth for 345 more years of the Kali-yuga.

Verse 20; The last of the Kāṇvas, Suśarmā, will be murdered by his own servant, Balī, a low-class śūdra of the Andhra race. This most degraded Maharaja Balī will have control over the earth for some time.

Verses 21-26; The brother of Balī, named Krishna, will become the next ruler of the earth. His son will be Śāntakarṇa and his son will be Paurṇamāsa. The son of Paurṇamāsa will be Lambodara, who will father Maharaja Cibilaka. From Cibilaka will come Meghasvāti, whose son will be Aṭamāna. The son of Aṭamāna will be Aniṣṭakarmā. His son will be Hāleya and his son will be Talaka. The son of Talaka will be Purīṣabhīru and following him Sunandana will become king. Sunandana will be followed by Cakora and the eight Bahus, among whom Śivasvāti will be a great subduer of enemies. The son of Śivasvāti will be Gomatī. His son will be Purīmān, whose son will be Medaśirā. His son will be Śivaskanda and his son will be Yajñaśrī. The son of Yajñaśrī will be Vijaya, who will have two sons, Candravijña and Lomadhi. These thirty kings will enjoy sovereignty over the earth for a total of 456 years, O favourite son of the Kurus.

Verse 27; Then will follow seven kings of the Ābhīra race from the city of Avabhṛti and then ten Gardabhīs. After them, sixteen kings of the Kaṅkas will rule and will be known for their excessive greed.

Verse 28; Eight Yavanas will then take power, followed by fourteen Turuṣkas, ten Guruṇḍas and eleven kings of the Maula dynasty.

Verses 29-31; These Ābhīras, Gardabhīs and Kaṅkas will enjoy the earth for 1,099 years and the Maulas will rule for 300 years. When all of them have died off there will appear in the city of Kilakilā a dynasty of kings consisting of Bhūtananda, Vaṅgiri, Śiśunandi, Śiśunandi's brother Yaśonandi and Pravīraka. These kings of Kilakilā will hold sway for a total of 106 years.

Verses 32-33; The Kilakilās will be followed by their thirteen sons, the Bāhlikas and after them King Puṣpamitra, his son Durmitra, seven Andhras, seven Kauśalas and also kings of the Viḍūra and Niṣadha provinces will separately rule in different parts of the world.

Verse 34; There will then appear a king of the Māgadhas named Viśvasphūrji, who will be like another Purañjaya. He will turn all the civilized classes into low-class, uncivilized men in the same category as the Pulindas, Yadus and Madrakas.

Verse 35; Foolish King Viśvasphūrji will maintain all the citizens in ungodliness and will use his power to completely disrupt the Kshatriya order. From his capital of Padmavati, he will rule that part of the earth extending from the source of the Ganga to Prayag.

Verse 36; At that time the Brahmins of such provinces as Saurashtra, Avanti, Ābhīra, Śūra, Arbuda and Mālava will forget all their regulative principles and the members of the royal order in these places will become no better than fourth-class.

Verse 37; The land along the Sindhu River, as well as the districts of Chandrabhaga, Kanti and Kashmira, will be ruled by fourth-class, fallen brahmins and meat-eaters. Having given up the path of Vedic civilization, they will have lost all spiritual strength.

Verse 38; There will be many such uncivilized kings ruling at the same time, O King Parikshit and they will all be uncharitable, possessed of fierce tempers and great devotees of irreligion and falsity.

Verses 39-40; These barbarians in the guise of kings will devour the citizenry, murdering innocent women, children, cows and brahmins and coveting the wives and property of other men. They will be erratic in their moods, have little strength of character and be very short-lived. Indeed, not purified by any Vedic rituals and lacking in the practice of regulative principles, they will be completely covered by the modes of passion and ignorance.

Verse 41; The citizens governed by these low-class kings will imitate the character, behavior and speech of their rulers. Harassed by their leaders and by each other, they will all suffer ruination.

Chapter Two – The Symptoms of Kali-Yuga

This chapter relates that, when the bad qualities of the Age of Kali will increase to an intolerable level, the Supreme Personality of Godhead will descend (incarnate) as Kalki to destroy those who are fixed in irreligion. After that, a new Satya-yuga will begin.

As the Age of Kali progresses, all good qualities of men diminish and all impure qualities increase. Atheistic systems of so-called religion will become predominant, replacing the codes of Vedic law. The kings will be just like highway bandits, the people in general become dedicated to low occupations and all the social classes become just like fourth-class. All cows will become like goats, all spiritual hermitages will be like materialistic homes and family ties will not extend no further than the immediate relationship of marriage.

When the Age of Kali has almost ended, the Supreme Personality of Godhead will incarnate. He will appear in the village Shambhala, in the home of the exalted Brahmin Viṣṇuyaśā and will take the name Kalki. He will mount His horse Devadatta and, taking His sword in hand, will roam about the earth killing millions of bandits in the guise of kings. Then the signs of the next Satya-yuga will begin to appear. When the Moon, Sun and the planet Brhaspati (Jupitar) enter simultaneously into one constellation and conjoin in the lunar mansion Puṣyā, Satya-yuga will begin. In the order of Satya, Tretā,

Dvāpara and Kali, the cycle of four ages again will start rotating in the society of living entities in this universe.

The chapter ends with a brief description of the future dynasties of the sun and moon coming from Vaivasvata Manu in the next Satya-yuga. Even now two saintly kshatriyas are living who at the end of this Kali-yuga will reinitiate the pious dynasties of the sun-God, Vivasvān and the moon-God, Candra. One of these kings is Devāpi, a brother of Mahārāja

Verse 1; Śukadeva Gosvāmī said; Then, O King! religion, truthfulness, cleanliness, tolerance, mercy, duration of life, physical strength and memory will all diminish day by day because of the powerful influence of the Age of Kali.

Verse 2; In Kali-yuga, wealth alone will be considered the sign of a man's good birth, proper behavior and fine qualities. And law and justice will be applied only on the basis of one's power.

Verse 3; Men and women will live together merely because of superficial attraction and success in business will depend on deceit. Womanliness and manliness will be judged according to one's expertise in sex and a man will be known as a brahmin just by his wearing a thread.

Verse 4; A person's spiritual position will be ascertained merely according to external symbols and on that same basis people will change from one spiritual order to the next. A person's propriety will be seriously questioned if he does not earn a good living. And one who is very clever at juggling words will be considered a learned scholar.

Verse 5; A person will be judged unholy if he does not have money and hypocrisy will be accepted as virtue. Marriage will be arranged simply by verbal agreement and a person will think he is fit to appear in public if he has merely taken a bath.

Verse 6; A sacred place will be taken to consist of no more than a reservoir of water located at a distance and beauty will be thought to depend on one's hairstyle. Filling the belly will become the goal of life and one who is audacious will be accepted as truthful. He who can maintain a family will be regarded as an expert man and the principles of religion will be observed only for the sake of reputation.

Verse 7; As the earth thus becomes crowded with a corrupt population, whoever among any of the social classes shows himself to be the strongest will gain political power.

Verse 8; Losing their wives and properties to such avaricious and merciless rulers, who will behave no better than ordinary thieves, the citizens will flee to the mountains and forests.

Verse 9; Harassed by famine and excessive taxes, people will resort to eating leaves, roots, flesh, wild honey, fruits, flowers and seeds. Struck by drought, they will become completely ruined.

Verse 10; The citizens will suffer greatly from cold, wind, heat, rain and snow. They will be further tormented by quarrels, hunger, thirst, disease and severe anxiety.

Verse 11; The maximum duration of life for human beings in Kali-yuga will become fifty years.

Verses 12-16; By the time the Age of Kali ends, the bodies of all creatures will be greatly reduced in size and the religious principles of followers of varnashrama will be ruined. The path of the Vedas will be completely forgotten in human society and so-called religion will be mostly atheistic. The kings will mostly be thieves, the occupations of men will be stealing, lying and needless violence and all the social classes will be reduced to the lowest level of fourth-class. Cows will be like goats, spiritual hermitages will be no different from mundane houses and family ties will extend no further than the immediate bonds of marriage. Most plants and herbs will be tiny and all trees will appear like dwarf śamī trees. Clouds will be full of lightning, homes will be devoid of piety and all human beings will have become like asses. At that time, the Supreme Personality of Godhead will appear on the earth. Acting with the power of pure spiritual goodness, He will rescue eternal religion.

Verse 17; Lord Viṣṇu — the Supreme Personality of Godhead, the spiritual master of all moving and non-moving living beings and the Supreme Soul of all — takes birth to protect the principles of religion and to relieve His saintly devotees from the reactions of material work.

Verse 18; Lord Kalki will appear in the home of the most eminent brahmin of Śambhala village, the great soul Viṣṇuyaśā.

Verses 19-20; Lord Kalki, the Lord of the universe, will mount His swift horse Devadatta and, sword in hand, travel over the earth exhibiting his eight mystic opulences and eight special qualities of Godhead. Displaying His unequaled effulgence and riding with great speed, He will kill by the millions those thieves who have dared dress as kings.

Verse 21; After all the impostor kings have been killed, the residents of the cities and towns will feel the breezes carrying the most sacred fragrance of the sandalwood paste and other decorations of Lord Vāsudeva and their minds will thereby become transcendentally pure.

Verse 22; When Lord Vāsudeva, the Supreme Personality of Godhead, appears in their hearts in His transcendental form of goodness, the remaining citizens will abundantly repopulate the earth.

Verse 23; When the Supreme Lord has appeared on earth as Kalki, the maintainer of religion, Satya-yuga will begin and human society will bring forth progeny in the mode of goodness.

Verse 24; When the moon, the sun and Brhaspati are together in the constellation Karkaṭa and all three enter simultaneously into the lunar mansion Puṣyā — at that exact moment the age of Satya, or Kṛta, will begin.

Verse 25; Thus, I have described all the kings — past, present and future — who belong to the dynasties of the sun and the moon.

Verse 26; From your birth up to the coronation of King Nanda, 1,150 years will pass.

Verses 27-28; Of the seven stars forming the constellation of the seven sages, Pulaha and Kratu are the first to rise in the night sky. If a line running north and south were drawn through their midpoint, whichever of the lunar mansions this line passes through is said to be the ruling asterism of the constellation for that time. The Seven Sages will remain connected with that particular lunar mansion for one hundred human years. Currently, during your lifetime, they are situated in the nakshatra called Magha.

Verse 29; The Supreme Lord, Viṣṇu, is brilliant like the sun and is known as Krishna. When He returned to the spiritual sky, Kali entered this world and people then began to take pleasure in sinful activities.

Verse 30; As long as Lord Śrī Krishna, the husband of the goddess of fortune, touched the earth with His lotus feet, Kali was powerless to subdue this planet.

Verse 31; When the constellation of the seven sages is passing through the lunar mansion Magha, the Age of Kali begins. It comprises twelve hundred years of the demigods.

Verse 32; When the great sages of the Saptarishi constellation pass from Magha to Pūrvāsāḍhā, Kali will have his full strength, beginning from King Nanda and his dynasty.

Verse 33; Those who scientifically understand the past declare that on the very day that Lord Śrī Krishna departed for the spiritual world, the influence of the Age of Kali began.

Verse 34; After the one thousand celestial years of Kali-yuga, the Satya-yuga will manifest again. At that time the minds of all men will become self-effulgent.

Verse 35; Thus, I have described the royal dynasty of Manu, as it is known on this earth. One can similarly study the history of the Vaisyas, fourth-class and brahmins living in the various ages.

Verse 36; These personalities, who were great souls, are now known only by their names. They exist only in accounts from the past and only their fame remains on the earth.

Verse 37; Devāpi, the brother of Mahārāja Santana and Maru, the descendant of Ikṣvāku, both possess great mystic strength and are living even now in the village of Kalāpa.

Verse 38; At the end of the Age of Kali, these two kings, having received instruction directly from the Supreme Personality of

Godhead, Vāsudeva, will return to human society and reestablish the eternal religion of man, characterized by the divisions of varṇa and āśrama, just as it was before.

Verse 39; The cycle of four ages — Satya, Tretā, Dvāpara and Kali — continues perpetually among living beings on this earth, repeating the same general sequence of events.

Verse 40; My dear King Parikshit! all these kings I have described, as well as all other human beings, come to this earth and stake their claims, but ultimately, they all must give up this world and meet their destruction.

Verse 41; Even though a person's body may now have the designation 'king', in the end its name will be 'worms', 'stool' or 'ashes'. What can a person who injures other living beings for the sake of his body know about his own self-interest, since his activities are simply leading him to hell?

Verse 42; [The materialistic king thinks;] "This unbounded earth was held by my predecessors and is now under my sovereignty. How can I arrange for it to remain in the hands of my sons, grandsons and other descendants?"

Verse 43; Although the foolish accept the body made of earth, water and fire as 'me' and this earth as 'mine', in every case they have ultimately abandoned both their body and the earth and passed away into oblivion.

Verse 44; My dear King Parikshit, all these kings who tried to enjoy the earth by their strength were reduced by the force of time to nothing more than historical accounts.

Note; The word 'king' in the above verses may equally be treated as rulers/ ministers in this current democratic set-up.

Shrimad Devī Bhāgavata 12th *Kāṇḍa* – 9th Chapter

Once, on account of an evil turn of Fate (Karma) of the human beings, Indra did not rain on this earth for fifteen years. Owing to want of rain, the famine appeared horribly and almost all the beings lost their lives. No one could count in every house the number of the dead persons.

Out of hunger the people began to eat horses. Some began to eat bears and pigs, some began to eat the dead bodies while some others carried on any how their lives. The people were so much distressed with hunger that the mother did not refrain from eating baby children and the husband did not refrain from eating his wife.

The age of Kali deludes the people and draws away their minds from reciting the Gayatri mantra save a few of them. Hence, they will have to remain in Kumbheebhaga hell upto the time when Sri Krishna takes his incarnation.

After Sri Krishna ascended to the Vaikunta, when the Kali age came, those cursed people got out of the Kumbheebhaka hell and took their births in this earth as Brahmins, devoid of the three Sandhyas, devoid of the devotion to Gayatri Devi, devoid of faith in the Vedas, advocating the heretics' opinion and unwilling to perform Agnihotra and other religious sacrifices and duties and they were devoid of Svadha and Svaha.

Note; Both Swada Devi and Swaha Devi are the wives of Lord Agni. Swada Devi takes the offerings made by those performing the Homam in Agni to the Pitrus and Swaha Devi to the Devas.

They forgot entirely the Unmanifested Moola Prakrti Bhagavati. Some of them began to mark on their bodies various heretical signs, like Taptamudra; some became Kapalikas; some became Kaulas; some Bauddhas and some Jains. Many of them, though learned, became lewd and addicted to other's wives and engaged themselves in vain and bad disputations.

Shrimad Bhagavad Gita – Part of Maha Bharatha
Chapter 8; Attaining the Supreme

The duration of the material universe is limited. It is manifested in cycles of kalpas. A kalpa is a day of Brahma and one day of Brahma consists of a thousand cycles of four yugas or ages: Satya, Treta, Dvapara and Kali. The cycle of Satya is characterized by virtue, wisdom and religion, there being practically no ignorance and vice and the yuga lasts 1,728,000 years. In the Treta-yuga vice is introduced and this yuga lasts 1,296,000 years. In the Dvapara-yuga there is an even greater decline in virtue and religion, vice increasing and this yuga lasts 864,000 years. And finally in Kali-yuga (the yuga we have now been experiencing over the past 5,000 years) there is an abundance of strife, ignorance, irreligion and vice, true virtue being practically nonexistent and this yuga lasts 432,000 years.

In Kali-yuga vice increases to such a point that at the termination of the yuga the Supreme Lord Himself appears as the Kalki incarnation, vanquishes the demons, saves His devotees and commences another Satya-yuga. Then the process is set rolling again. These four yugas, rotating a thousand times, comprise one day of Brahma, the creator god and the same number comprise one night. Brahma lives one hundred of such 'years' and then another Brahma originates.

These "hundred years" by earth calculations total to 311 trillion and 40 million earth years. By these calculations the life of Brahma seems fantastic and interminable, but from the viewpoint of eternity it is as brief as a lightning flash. In the causal ocean there are innumerable Brahmas rising and disappearing like bubbles in the Atlantic. Brahma and his creation are all part of the material universe and therefore they are in constant flux.

In the material universe not even, Brahma is free from the process of birth, old age, disease and death. Brahma, however, is directly engaged in the service of the Supreme Lord in the management of this universe-therefore he at once attains liberation. Elevated sannyasis are promoted to Brahma's particular planet, Brahma Loka, which is the highest planet in the material universe and which survives all the heavenly planets in the upper strata of the planetary system, but in due course Brahma and all inhabitants of Brahma Loka are subject to death, according to the law of material nature.

Adyatma Ramayana Mahatmya – Verses 9 to 15

The Adyatma Ramayana is a book written by Valmiki in Samskrutam, later than the original Ramayana written by Valmiki. (Whether both the Valmikis are one and the same is a disputable topic). It describes the deeds of Rama in a spiritual way. It symbolises the journey of the soul and helps seekers realise the identity of their soul. It consists of seven kandas – Bala, Ayodhya, Aranya, Kishkindha, Sundara, Yuddha and Uttara. Altogether, there are 4,242 shlokas. There is also a Mahatmya chapter of 60 verses which is from Brahmanda Purana. This describes the greatness of Adyatma Ramayana. Shlokas 9 to 15 of this Mahatmya talks about the Kali era very much in advance.

These verses are in the form of conversation between the great sage Narada and his father Brahma. Narada asked Brahma – Sir! What are the auspicious actions? What are the ones that can cause evil? You have already told me about this. However, now I have doubts again. Even though it is a very secret matter, I ask you to have mercy on me and remove the doubts and grace me.

When the terrible Kali Yuga arrives, people will engage in sinful activities such as lying, immorality, slander, stealing other people's property and harassing others and will refrain from doing pious deeds. Besides that, they will also think that the body is the soul and will be absorbed in the pleasures of the body, will indulge in the lust of women and will not protect their parents, will be atheists and will behave like animals.

Moreover, the Brahmins will make a living by selling the Vedas. It may even happen that the Kshatriyas and Vaishyas will be negligent in performing their respective duties and the fourth class will insult the Brahmins. Further, women will also insult their husbands and move about without fear. Besides, they will be those who neglect elders, lose knowledge and commit unrighteousness without any hesitation.

Note; It is very clear, how accurate the prediction of Kali Yuga in Narada's statement is in the present days.

Narada stood there humbly saying – I am troubled by the worry of how these people will attain good fortune and I beg you to suggest some good remedy, for the people of Kali Yuga who are about to suffer from loss of knowledge. If there is any easy path to good fortune, please tell me and bless me.

In reply and as a therapy to this that the four-faced Brahma, spoke beautifully about the Adyatma Ramayana.

The above verses are all predictions of future Kali Yuga. But seemingly it is more of past history. Historians may also not be able to provide this much accurate names, years of ruling, etc. The sages' ability to predict the future with such a precision is truly astonishing. This is possible only because of their deep penance.

Sri Lalita Trishatee – 15th name – *Kalidoṣaharā* – *Srī Devī* eradicates all the evils inherent in *Kaliyuga* (era of *Kali*) such as atheism, agnosticism and useless debates/ arguments and establishes one-ness of all existence with Herself (*Advaita*) in the minds of deluded and confused people.

*****

Kaliviḍambana Stotram – An Understanding

1. Argumentative

Na Bhetavyaṃ Na Boddhavyaṃ Na Śrāvyaṃ Vādino Vacaḥ |
Jhaṭiti Prativaktavyaṃ Sabhāsu Vijigīṣubhiḥ ||

न भेतव्यं न बोद्धव्यं न श्राव्यं वादिनो वचः ।

झटिति प्रतिवक्तव्यं सभासु विजिगीषुभिः ॥

One who is desires of winning a debate in the court of a King need not be afraid of his opponent, nor should he try to listen or understand the points advanced by his opponent. Spontaneously he should speak up whatever comes to his mind. That will be the real qualification for winning a debate.

2. *Asambhramo Vilajjatvamavajñā Prativādini |*
Hāso Rājñaḥ Stavaśceti Pañcaite Jayahetavaḥ ||

असम्भ्रमो विलज्जत्वमवज्ञा प्रतिवादिनि । हासो राज्ञः स्तवश्चेति पञ्चैते जयहेतवः ॥

The essential qualities for winning a debate are having patience, without stage fear, giving up all senses of shame, insulting the opponent scholar, to laugh at the points advanced by such scholar finally keep praising the sponsor frequently during the course of the debate.

There are five ways by which one could win a debate in the court – not being panicky, letting go of shame, ignoring the opponent, laughing loudly and praising the king.

The contents of this verse are very much applicable to the current days, which we see in various debates telecast in television shows.

3. *Uccairudghoṣya Jetavyaṃ Madhyasthaścedapaṇḍitaḥ |*
Paṇḍito Yadi Tatraiva Pakṣapāto'dhiropyatām ||

उच्चैरुद्घोष्य जेतव्यं मध्यस्थश्चेदपण्डितः ।

पण्डितो यदि तत्रैव पक्षपातोऽधिरोप्यताम् ॥

During the course of the debate the debater should make noise, if the judge is not adequately knowledgeable in the subject. if the judge is a learned scholar, the debater should accuse him of partiality for that will be the surest way to win one's point of view in a debate. We know that this hymn describes the calamities of Kaliyuga. But the above three shlokas talk about debates and winning debates. What does this have to do with the calamities of Kali Yuga?

In earlier times, in earlier yugas, whatever the elders, parents or guru said, the younger ones would accept it as it is, without murmurings or asking any questions. But, in this era, in Kaliyuga, they raise questions like why, what, how, where, etc. It is not wrong to ask such questions. Knowledge expands only when we listen and search for the answers. But this can go into debate. Who said where and when – we need to find the evidence/ authority/ source for this. The above three shlokas are dedicated to seeking success in debates.

4. *Lobho Heturdhanaṃ Sādhyaṃ Dṛṣṭāntastu Purohitaḥ |*
Ātmotkarṣo Nigamanamanumāneṣvayaṃ Vidhiḥ ॥

लोभो हेतुर्धनं साध्यं दृष्टान्तस्तु पुरोहितः ।
आत्मोत्कर्षो निगमनमनुमानेष्वयं विधिः ॥

If one has a very strong craving for money, he should analyse and workout the means to earn. If he has a strong attachment to wealth, it would be easy for him to get it. For example, once a priest sets his eyes on money or smells it, he will not give up until he gets it. Therefore, it is to be concluded that if one desires money. he will get the same.

Greed is the cause and money is the goal. The Purohits or the Priests of Kaliyuga are examples of this. Growth of oneself is the final step in achieving the goal. This is the procedure of *Anumāna pramāṇam* in Kaliyuga.

5. *Abhyāsyaṃ Lajjamānena Tattvaṃ Jijñāsunā Ciram |*
Jigīṣunā Hriyaṃ Tyaktvā Kāryaḥ Kolāhalo Mahān ॥

अभ्यास्यं लज्जमानेन तत्त्वं जिज्ञासुना चिरम् ।

जिगीषुना हियं त्यक्त्वा कार्यः कोलाहलो महान् ॥

One who has sincerity in the acquisition of knowledge, he should pursue the same with humility. However, such an effort would take a lot of time. Instead, if one aspect to become an eminent scholar very quickly, he should, giving up all senses of shame, loudly proclaim and exhibit his limited knowledge in the given subject.

Furthermore, for those who wish to achieve great success (*jigīṣū*) in a debate, they must abandon all forms of shyness or hesitation (*hrī*). Instead, they should focus on creating a significant impact (*kolāhala*) through their actions characterized by dynamic and loud endeavors.

Here, '*Kōlāhala*' symbolises confidence. A person who speaks loudly in a debate often exudes confidence in their arguments, which can intimidate opponents and pave the way to victory.

Skill or knowledge (*abhyāsaḥ*) needs to be practiced diligently. The learner should study without any sense of shame. Those who desire victory must abandon shyness and make a significant noise about their affairs.

6.   Pandit/ teacher

Pāṭhanairgranthanirmāṇaiḥ Pratiṣṭhā Tāvadāpyate |
Evaṃ Ca Tathyavyutpattirāyuṣo'nte Bhavenna Vā ॥

पाठनैर्ग्रन्थनिर्माणैः प्रतिष्ठा तावदाप्यते ।
एवं च तथ्यव्युत्पत्तिरायुषोऽन्ते भवेन्न वा ॥

Teaching and writing books can bring recognition and fame in society, making people believe the person possess complete knowledge. However, true wisdom and understanding of the deeper truths require sincere self-reflection, which is often overlooked. In Kali Yuga, many focus on gaining prestige rather than pursuing genuine knowledge, making true wisdom increasingly rare.

A person may attain great fame and reputation by teaching others with his incomplete knowledge. He may also right books, compose works with his limited knowledge. It is a most important point as to whether he himself will acquire complete knowledge on that subject at least before the end of his lifetime?

7. *Stotāraḥ Ke Bhaviṣyanti Mūrkhasya Jagatītale |*
Na Stauti Cetsvayaṃ Ca Svaṃ Kadā Tasyāstu Nirvṛtiḥ ||

स्तोतारः के भविष्यन्ति मूर्खस्य जगतीतले ।

न स्तौति चेत्स्वयं च स्वं कदा तस्यास्तु निर्वृतिः ॥

Who will admire a fool on the earth? If he does not praise himself, when will there be any satisfaction for him? The irony of self-praise and the lack of genuine admiration for those, who do not possess true qualities worthy of praise. It is suggested that without self-praise, a fool will never achieve any sense of satisfaction, emphasising the emptiness of seeking admiration for unworthy traits.

8. *Vācyatāṃ Samayo'tītaḥ Spaṣṭamagre Bhaviṣyati |*
Iti Pāṭhayatāṃ Granthe Kāṭhinyaṃ Kutra Vartate ||

वाच्यतां समयोऽतीतः स्पष्टमग्रे भविष्यति ।

इति पाठयतां ग्रन्थे काठिन्यं कुत्र वर्तते ॥

During the course of teaching when a student asks some difficult question to a half-baked teacher, the teacher will give an evasive reply that it is getting late or the question will be answered later. After sometime the student himself would find an answer for the question. The teacher has not exhibited his ignorance. For such a teacher and student there could be nothing called difficult part of any subject.

"It's already time. Keep studying and things will become clearer in the future" – To those that teach their students in this manner, wherefore pain?

9. *Agatitvamatiśraddhā Jñānābhāsena Tṛptatā |*
Trayaḥ Śiṣyaguṇā Hyete Mūrkhācāryasya Bhāgyajāḥ ||

अगतित्वमतिश्रद्धा ज्ञानाभासेन तृप्तता ।

त्रयः शिष्यगुणा होते मूर्खाचार्यस्य भाग्यजाः ॥

For a student to reach a half-baked teacher there could be three reasons – 1. non availability of a better teacher 2. the student may have unquenchable thirst for knowledge and 3 being satisfied with whatever that half-baked teacher teaches him. How fortunate indeed is such a teacher!

10. *Yadi Na Kvāpi Vidyāyāṃ Sarvathā Kramate Matiḥ |*
Māntrikāstu Bhaviṣyāmo Yogino Yatayo'pi Vā ॥

यदि न क्वापि विद्यायां सर्वथा क्रमते मतिः ।
मान्त्रिकास्तु भविष्यामो योगिनो यतयोऽपि वा ॥

If for any reason, a person is not able to succeed in any field of study due to his dull intellect, he will become either a witch-craft or a yogi.

If we are so dumb-witted that nothing at all can stimulate our minds, we shall try these options – practicing witchcraft, becoming yogis or renouncing the world.

11. Magicians (Witchcrafts)

Avilambena Saṃsiddhau Māntrikairāpyate Yaśaḥ |
Vilambe Karmabāhulyaṃ Vikhyāpyāvāpyate Dhanam ॥

अविलम्बेन संसिद्धौ मान्त्रिकैराप्यते यशः ।
विलम्बे कर्मबाहुल्यं विख्याप्यावाप्यते धनम् ॥

The magicians (witchcrafts) will attain great fame, if their incantations give instant results. In cases where incantations take time to give results, they conduct elaborate rituals of Pooja, fire worship, etc. and through that earn a lot of fame and money. Either way, they stand benefited whether they succeed or fail in the rituals.

12. *Sukhaṃ Sukhiṣu Duḥkhe'pi Jīvanaṃ Duḥkhaśāliṣu |*
Anugrahāyate Yeṣāṃ Te Dhanyāḥ Khalu Māntrikāḥ ॥

सुखं सुखिषु दुःखेऽपि जीवनं दुःखशालिषु ।

अनुग्रहायते येषां ते धन्याः खलु मान्त्रिकाः ॥

The most fortunate mantrikas or magicians prescribe various religious rites to well off people and earn money. To those who are in difficulties, they would state that the problems would be resolved through rituals prescribed by them. Such magicians will always lead a steady life. How fortunate are they?

13. *Yāvadajñānato Maunamācāro Vā Vilakṣaṇaḥ |*
Tāvanmāhātmyarūpeṇa Paryavasyati Māntrike Aḥ ॥

यावदज्ञानतो मौनमाचारो वा विलक्षणः ।
तावन्माहात्म्यरूपेण पर्यवस्यति मान्त्रिके अः ॥

Keeping a vow of silence on account of ignorance and giving up the religious disciplines on account of the fact that they have attained proficiency in the Mantra Sadhana would be considered as natural traits of such mantrikas or magicians

14. Astrologer

Cārān Vicārya Daivajñairvaktavyaṃ Bhūbhujāṃ Phalam |
Grahacāraparijñānaṃ Teṣāmāvaśyakaṃ Yataḥ ॥

चारान् विचार्य दैवज्ञैर्वक्तव्यं भूभुजां फलम् ग्रहचारपरिज्ञानं तेषामावश्यकं यतः ॥

The Astrologer giving predictions to the king of the land or to anybody else, need to carefully go through the natal charts or horoscopes before giving his predictions. Otherwise, he may incur the king's wrath. But in this Kali yuga an astrologer who gives prediction to a man, will first find out the day-to-day status and activities of such a man his wealth conditions and only then he will give predictions. If the astrologer gathers beforehand all such information about the man, there is no need for him to see his horoscope or planetary movements.

15. *Putra Ityeva Pitari Kanyaketi Mātari |*
Garbhapraśneṣu Kathayan Daivajño Vijayī Bhavet ॥

पुत्र इत्येव पितरि कन्यकेति मातरि । गर्भप्रश्नेषु कथयन् दैवज्ञो विजयी भवेत् ॥

An astrologer will easily succeed in making a prediction when a pregnant woman asks about the sex of the to be born baby. He would say that it is a female child to the mother and it is a male child to the father. In any case his prediction is correct either with the mother or with the father and hence he will succeed.

16. *Āyuspraśne Dīrghamāyurvācyaṃ Mauhūrtikairjanaiḥ |*
Jīvanto Bahumanyante Mṛtāḥ Prakṣyanti Kaṃ Punaḥ ॥

आयुस्प्रश्ने दीर्घमायुर्वाच्यं मौहूर्तिकैर्जनैः ।
जीवन्तो बहुमन्यन्ते मृताः प्रक्ष्यन्ति कं पुनः ॥

To a person who asked the astrologer about how long he would live, the astrologer should promptly tell him that he will live a very long life. The astrologer should realise that only the persons who live long would pay for his services. The persons who have short lives will not come back to argue.

17. *Sarvaṃ Koṭidvayopetaṃ Sarvaṃ Kāladvayāvadhi |*
Sarvaṃ Vyāmiśramiva Ca Vaktavyaṃ Daivacintakaiḥ ॥

सर्वं कोटिद्वयोपेतं सर्वं कालद्वयावधि । सर्वं व्यामिश्रमिव च वक्तव्यं दैवचिन्तकैः ॥

An astrologer should give prediction to the seeker of his advice that the intended action of the seeker possibly may or may not workout. He should state that even if the action does not bear any fruits in the present time, it will work out in future.

18. *Nirdhanānāṃ Dhanāvāptiṃ Dhanināmadhikaṃ Dhanam |*
Bruvāṇāḥ Sarvathā Grāhyā Lokairjyautiṣikā Janāḥ ॥

निर्धनानां धनावाप्तिं धनिनामधिकं धनम् ।
ब्रुवाणाः सर्वथा ग्राह्या लोकैर्ज्यौतिषिका जनाः ॥

An astrologer should give prediction to a poor person that he would become rich and to a rich person that he would become richer. Only such an astrologer is respected by the people.

19. *Śatasya Lābhe Tāmbūlaṃ Sahasrasya Tu Bhojanam |*
Daivajñānāmupālambho Nityaḥ Kāryaviparyaye ||

शतस्य लाभे ताम्बूलं सहस्रस्य तु भोजनम् ।
दैवज्ञानामुपालम्भो नित्यः कार्यविपर्यये ॥

If the prediction of an astrologer comes true for 100 times, he will be rewarded with betel leaves as a mark of respect. If it has efficacy of 1,000 times, he will be honoured with a grand feast. However, if for some reason, his prediction fails, he will receive criticism as his reward.

20. *Api Sāgaraparyantā Vicetavyā Vasundharā |*
Deśo Hyaratnimātre'pi Nāsti Daivajñavarjitaḥ ||

अपि सागरपर्यन्ता विचेतव्या वसुन्धरा । देशो ह्यरत्निमात्रेऽपि नास्ति दैवज्ञवर्जितः ॥

In the vast expanse of this earth which has only the ocean as its border, astrologers are seen everywhere. The entire landscape of the earth is filled without even a small gap. Most of the astrologers are without much of knowledge in astrology. It is very difficult to find out an astrologer with complete knowledge.

21. *Vārān Ke Cidgrahān Ke Citke Cidṛkṣāṇi Jānate |*
Tritayaṃ Ye Vijānanti Te Vācaspatayaḥ Svayam ||

वारान् के चिद्ग्रहान् के चित्के चिदृक्षाणि जानते ।
त्रितयं ये विजानन्ति ते वाचस्पतयः स्वयम् ॥

Among the astrologers some know only the names of the days of the weeks, some only know the names of the planets and some only know that names of the stars. Yet they would shine as great astrologers. But the astrologers who know all the above will shine as lords of astrology. Such astrologers are very few and very rare to find out.

22. *Naimittikāḥ Svapnadṛśo Devatānāṃ [[Amī Trayaḥ]]* |
Nisargaśatravaḥ Sṛṣṭā Daivajñānāmamī Trayaḥ ‖ ‖

नैमित्तिकाः स्वप्नदृशो देवतानां [[अमी त्रयः]] ।
निसर्गशत्रवः सृष्टा दैवज्ञानाममी त्रयः ॥

These astrologers have three types of natural enemies. Those who give prediction on the basis of omens. Those give prediction on the basis of dreams. And those who give prediction by propitiating gods and goddess.

23. Doctors

Svasthairasādhyarogaiśca Jantubhirnāsti Kiṃ Cana |
Kātarā Dīrgharogāśca Bhiṣajāṃ Bhāgyahetavaḥ ‖

स्वस्थैरसाध्यरोगैश्च जन्तु भिर्नास्ति किं चन ।
कातरा दीर्घरोगाश्च भिषजां भाग्यहेतवः ॥

Persons who are very healthy or who have incurable diseases are of no use to any physician. The persons for martially scared of any disease or who have terminal diseases are the priced possessions of a physician, obtained due to the merits of his past births.

24. *Nātidhairyaṃ Pradātavyaṃ Nātibhītiśca Rogiṇi* |
Naiścintyānnādime Dānaṃ Nairāśyādeva Nāntime ‖

नातिधैर्यं प्रदातव्यं नातिभीतिश्च रोगिणि ।
नैश्चिन्त्यान्नादिमे दानं नैराश्यादेव नान्तिमे ॥

A physician should not give excessive confidence for the sick patients. If they do, then those patients would desert him and avoid giving him the fees. Similarly, if the physician, scares a patient in the name of the diseases then the patients may avoid him out of dejection and not pay him also.

25. *Bhaiṣajyaṃ Tu Yathākāmaṃ Pathyaṃ Tu Kaṭhinaṃ Vadet |*
Ārogyaṃ Vaidyamāhātmyādanyathātvamapathyataḥ ॥

भैषज्यं तु यथाकामं पथ्यं तु कठिनं वदेत् ।
आरोग्यं वैद्यमाहात्म्यादन्यथात्वमपथ्यतः ॥

A physician should give a very difficult prescription to his patient for a given disease, as it appears in his mind. If the disease gets cured, the physician would attribute the cure to the suggested remedy. For some reason, the disease is not cured, he would maintain that it is due to the patient not following the prescription properly.

26. *Nidānaṃ Roganāmāni Sātmyāsātmye Cikitsitam |*
Sarvamapyupadekṣyanti Rogiṇaḥ Sadane Striyaḥ ॥

निदानं रोगनामानि सात्म्यासात्म्ये चिकित्सितम् ।
सर्वमप्युपदेक्ष्यन्ति रोगिणः सदने स्त्रियः ॥

If the physician comes home to treat the patient, the ladies in the house themselves, would educate him about the disease, why the patient caught it and how it should be cured, etc.

27. *Jṛmbhamāṇeṣu Rogeṣu Mriyamāṇeṣu Jantuṣu |*
Rogatattveṣu Śanakairvyutpadyante Cikitsakāḥ ॥

जृम्भमाणेषु रोगेषु म्रियमाणेषु जन्तुषु ।रोगतत्त्वेषु शनकैर्व्युत्पद्यन्ते चिकित्सकाः ॥

Some physicians learn through the treatment of a disease, either at the time when the disease intensities in the patient or when the patient finally dies. In other words, they learn the real nature of disease only at the cost of the life of the patient.

28. *Pravartanārthamārambhe Madhye Tvauṣadhahetave |*
Bahumānārthamante Ca Jihīrṣanti Cikitsakāḥ ॥

प्रवर्तनार्थमारम्भे मध्ये त्वौषधहेतवे । बहुमानार्थमन्ते च जिहीर्षन्ति चिकित्सकाः ॥

Some physicians try to fleece money from the patients, initially in the name of treatment, then during the course of the treatment for medicines and finally towards their fees.

29. *Lipsamāneṣu Vaidyeṣu Cirādāsādya Roginam |*
Dāyādāḥ Samprarohanti Daivajñā Māntrikā Api ||

लिप्समानेषु वैद्येषु चिरादासाद्य रोगिणम् ।
दायादाः सम्प्ररोहन्ति दैवज्ञा मान्त्रिका अपि ॥

After a lot of perseverance and expectation, when a physician gets a patient and attempts to fleece him, the astrologers and magicians suddenly appear as competitors, to wrest the money from the patient.

30. *Rogasyopakrame Sāntvaṃ Madhye Kiṃ Ciddhanavyayaḥ |*
Śanairanādarassāntau Snāto Vaidyaṃ Na Paśyati ||

रोगस्योपक्रमे सान्त्वं मध्ये किं चिद्धनव्ययः ।
शनैरनादरश्शान्तौ स्नातो वैद्यं न पश्यति ॥

When a person is sick, initially he tactfully and reluctantly interacts with the physician and after a while he spends some money towards medication. Once he is totally cured of the disease, he will never see that physician afterwards for fear of being robbed off his money. he does not set his foot or head in the direction of the physician.

31. *Daivajñatvaṃ Māntrikatā Bhaiṣajyaṃ Cāṭukauśalam |*
Ekaikamarthalābhāya Dvitriyogastu Durlabhaḥ ||

दैवज्ञत्वं मान्त्रिकता भैषज्यं चाटुकौशलम् ।एकैकमर्थलाभाय द्वित्रियोगस्तु दुर्लभः ॥

Being an astrologer or magician or physician or a person with the gift of gab – all these are money making ways. Of these, it is very rare to come across one person, who has more than one of these qualifications.

32. *Anṛtaṃ Cāṭuvādaśca Dhanayogo Mahānayam |*

Satyaṃ Vaiduṣyamityeṣa Yogo Dāridryakārakaḥ ॥

अनृतं चाटुवादश्च धनयोगो महानयम् ।सत्यं वैदुष्यमित्येष योगो दारिद्रयकारकः ॥

Uttering lies and speaking in an enticing method are the ways to become rich. Being honest and being a very big scholar are the sure passport to poverty.

33. Poets

Kātaryaṃ Durvinītattvaṃ Kārpaṇyamavivekatām |
Sarvaṃ Mārjanti Kavayaḥ Śālīnāṃ Muṣṭikiṅkarāḥ ॥

कातर्यं दुर्विनीतत्त्वं कार्पण्यमविवेकताम् ।
सर्वं मार्जन्ति कवयः शालीनां मुष्टिकिङ्कराः ॥

Sycophantic poets, for the sake of livelihood and earning enough money, glorify the bad quality of a person, in that process they themselves rub off the weaknesses of that person such as fear miserliness, ego and ignorance.

34. *Na Kāraṇamapekṣante Kavayaḥ Stotumudyatāḥ* |
Kiṃ Cidastuvatāṃ Teṣāṃ Jihvā Phuraphurāyate ॥

न कारणमपेक्षन्ते कवयः स्तोतुमुद्घताः ।किं चिदस्तुवतां तेषां जिह्वा फुरफुरायते ॥

Sycophantic poets, praise others without having any reason. For some time, if they do not praise anyone their tongues will have an itching sensation.

35. *Stutaṃ Stuvanti Kavayo Na Svato Guṇadarśinaḥ* |
Kītaḥ Kaścidalirnāma Kiyatī Tatra Varṇanā ॥

स्तुतं स्तुवन्ति कवयो न स्वतो गुणदर्शिनः ।
कीतः कश्चिदलिर्नाम कियती तत्र वर्णना ॥

Poets always glorify what others had already done and they do not speak about any new subject. Even though a bee is a small creature there is not a single poet who has not sung about it.

The poets who are devoid of imagination and originality are derided here.

36. *Ekaiva Kavitā Puṃsāṃ Grāmāyāśvāya Hastine |*
Antato'nnāya Vastrāya Tāmbūlāya Ca Kalpate ‖

एकैव कविता पुंसां ग्रामायाश्वाय हस्तिने ।
अन्ततोऽन्नाय वस्त्राय ताम्बूलाय च कल्पते ॥

In this world poems are composed for gaining popularity or getting patronage from a rich man or king – either an elephant or horse or cows or at least only food, clothes, betel leaves etc. It is traditional custom to honour poets with betel leaves along with rich gifts after rich repast.

37. *Śabdākhyamaparaṃ Brahma Sandarbheṇa Pariṣkṛtam |*
Vikrīyate Katipayairvṛthānyairviniyujyate ‖

शब्दाख्यमपरं ब्रह्म सन्दर्भेण परिष्कृतम् । विक्रीयते कतिपयैर्वृथान्यैर्विनियुज्यते ॥

Although endowed with poetic excellence and felicity of expressions of language, some poets fritter away the same in a wrongful way or uses the same for praising undeserving persons. That is singing the glory of undeserving people.

38. *Varṇayanti Narābhāsān Vāṇīṃ Labdhvāpi Ye Janāḥ |*
Labdhvāpi Kāmadhenuṃ Te Lāṅgale Viniyuñjate ‖

वर्णयन्ति नराभासान् वाणीं लब्ध्वापि ये जनाः ।
लब्ध्वापि कामधेनुं ते लाङ्गले विनियुञ्जते ॥

Some poets, inspite of being endowed with poetic excellence with the grace of Goddess of knowledge, use that gift for praising undeserving lowly people. They are like those who are bestowed with Kamadhenu, the wish yielding cow, use it for ploughing the field. Whose loss, is it?

39. *Praśaṃsanto Narābhāsān Pralapanto'nyathānyathā |*

Katham Tarantu Kavayaḥ Kāmapāramyavādinaḥ ॥

प्रशंसन्तो नराभासान् प्रलपन्तोऽन्यथान्यथा ।कथं तरन्तु कवयः कामपारम्यवादिनः ॥

Some poets, out of sycophancy, sing the glory of low-level undeserving people, for the sake of earning money. How are these people going to cross the ocean of desires?

40. *Yatsandarbhe Yadullekhe Yadvyaṅgye Nibhṛtaṃ Manaḥ* |
Samādherapi Tajjyāyāḥ Śaṅkaro Yadi Varṇyate ॥

यत्सन्दर्भे यदुल्लेखे यद्व्यङ्ग्ये निभृतं मनः ।
समाधेरपि तज्ज्यायाः शङ्करो यदि वर्ण्यते ॥

If one's mind is absorbed deeply in the composition and description of poetry and if, Lord Shiva happens to be the subject of such poetry that state of mind will indeed be better than the real state of Samadhi, the blissful state.

Bandhavaḥ – बन्धवः – Relatives

41. Family Members
Gṛhiṇī Bhaginī Tasyāḥ Śvaśurau Śyāla Ityapi |
Prāṇinām Kalinā Sṛṣṭāḥ Pañca Prāṇā Ime'pare ॥

गृहिणी भगिनी तस्याः श्वशुरौ श्याल इत्यपि ।
प्राणिनां कलिना सृष्टाः पञ्च प्राणा इमेऽपरे ॥

Lord Brahma the creator has granted 5 *pranas* to human beings viz., *Pranan, Apanan, Vyanan, Udanan* and *Samanan*. In addition to this, *Kali Purusha* has granted 5 more *pranas* namely wife, her sister, her brother, father-in-law and mother-in-law.

42. *Jāmātaro Bhāgineyā Mātulā Dārabāndhavāḥ* |
Ajñātā Eva Gṛhiṇām Bhakṣyantyākhuvadgṛhe ॥

जामातरो भागिनेया मातुला दारबान्धवाः । अज्ञाता एव गृहिणां भक्ष्यन्त्याखुवद्गृहे ॥

In one's own house, son in law, nephews, cousins, wife's relatives and all, will eat slowly into his wealth like rats without his knowledge.

43. *Mātulasya Balaṃ Mātā Jāmāturduhitā Balam |*
Śvaśurasya Balaṃ Bhāryā Svayamevātitherbalam ||

मातुलस्य बलं माता जामातुर्दुहिता बलम् ।
श्वशुरस्य बलं भार्या स्वयमेवातिथेर्बलम् ॥

For one's maternal uncle, who has come to stay with him, his mother will be the strength (since she will automatically take care of her brother). For one's son-in-law, his daughter will be the strength (she will take care of her husband). For his father-in-law, his wife (she will take care of her father) and to a guest he himself is the strength.

44. Son-in-law

Jāmāturvakratā Tāvadyāvacchyālasya Bālatā |
Prabudhyamāne Sāralyaṃ Prabuddhe'smin Palāyanam ||

जामातुर्वक्रता तावद्यावच्छ्यालस्य बालता ।
प्रबुध्यमाने सारल्यं प्रबुद्धेऽस्मिन् पलायनम् ॥

As long as his brother-in-law is childish and innocent a son-in-law will be cunning and smart. But he will change, when his brother-in-law starts understanding his mischiefs. He will finally run away from that house when his brother-in-law starts exposing him.

45. *Bhāryā Jyeṣṭhā Śiśuḥ Śyālaḥ Śvaśrūḥ Svātantryavartinī |*
Śvaśurastu Pravāsīti Jāmāturbhāgyadhoraṇī ||

भार्या ज्येष्ठा शिशुः श्यालः श्वश्रूः स्वातन्त्र्यवर्तिनी ।
श्वशुरस्तु प्रवासीति जामातुर्भाग्यधोरणी ॥

Only that son-in-law is lucky, whose wife is the eldest child in her family. In that case, his brother-in-law will be a small child. His mother-in-law acts independently and father-in-law has gone on long voyage or tour. Such a son-in-law can rule that house to his heart's delight.

46. *Bhūṣaṇairvāsanaiḥ Pātraiḥ Putrāṇāmupalālanaiḥ |*
Sakṛdāgatya Gacchantī Kanyā Nirmārṣṭi Mandiram ॥

भूषणैर्वासनैः पात्रैः पुत्राणामुपलालनैः ।
सकृदागत्य गच्छन्ती कन्या निर्मार्ष्टि मन्दिरम् ॥

When a married woman visits her father's place, she almost empties that house by taking back with her rich clothes, ornaments and other small small things for the children.

47. *Gṛhiṇī Svajanaṃ Vakti Śuṣkāhāraṃ Mitāśanam |*
Patipakṣyāṃstu Bahvāśān Kṣīrapāṃstaskarānapi ॥

गृहिणी स्वजनं वक्ति शुष्काहारं मिताशनम् ।
पतिपक्ष्यांस्तु बह्वाशान् क्षीरपांस्तस्करानपि ॥

A housewife always complaints that when her relatives visit the house, they have simple food. Whereas when her husband's relations visit, they always eat rich food including healthy milk, curd, etc. and that they also steal the food and other items when they go back.

48. *Bhārye Dve Putraśālinyau Bhaginī Pativarjitā |*
Aśrāntakalaho Nāma Yogo'yaṃ Gṛhamedhinām ॥

भार्ये द्वे पुत्रशालिन्यौ भगिनी पतिवर्जिता ।
अश्रान्तकलहो नाम योगोऽयं गृहमेधिनाम् ॥

Some husbands have a luck called "endless fighting Yogam". They are blessed with this yoga when they have two wives and in addition a sister who is either a widow or a diverse. All these live together in the same house.

49. *Bhārye Dve Bahavaḥ Putrā Dāridryaṃ Rogasambhavaḥ |*
Jīrṇau Ca Mātāpitarāvekaikaṃ Narakādhikam ॥

भार्ये द्वे बहवः पुत्रा दारिद्र्यं रोगसम्भवः ।जीर्णौ च मातापितरावेकैकं नरकाधिकम् ॥

A husband who has one more of the following – two wives, countless children, poverty, sufferings due to disease and aged parents, will undergo misery that is equivalent to a hell.

Versus 41 to 49 might have been composed by the poet keeping in view of the social structure that was prevalent during his time when polygamy was common and joint family system was most prevalent everywhere.

Uttamarṇāḥ – उत्तमऋणाः – Lender

50. *Smṛte Sīdanti Gātrāṇi Dṛṣṭe Prajñā Vinaśyati |*
Aho Mahadidaṃ Bhūtamuttamarṇābhiśābdhitam ॥

स्मृते सीदन्ति गात्राणि दृष्टे प्रज्ञा विनश्यति ।
अहो महदिदं भूतमुत्तमऋणाभिशाब्धितम् ॥

A debtor is mortally shaken to his core, at the very thought or mention of the name of the creditor, like the name of a ghost was mentioned. At the very sight of the creditor his entrails are drawn out. What a wonder!

In the Ramayana, Ravana lost to Rama the first time and was returning. Rama also said "Leave today and come back tomorrow". While describing the state in which his head was bowed, *Kambar* mentioned "The Sri Lankan King was troubled like a creditor".

51. *Antako'pi Hi Jantūnāmantakālamapekṣate |*
Na Kālaniyamaḥ Kaściduttamārṇasya Vidyate ॥

अन्तकोऽपि हि जन्तूनामन्तकालमपेक्षते । न कालनियमः कश्चिदुत्तमार्णस्य विद्यते ॥

Yama, The Lord of Death, always waits for the last moment, till the end of the life of a person's scheduled time, before he takes of the life. But a creditor takes of the life of debtor, follows no rule as regards time.

52. *Na Paśyāmo Mukhe Daṃṣṭrāṃ Na Pāśaṃ Vā Karāñjale |*
Uttamārṇamavekṣyaiva Tathāpyudvejite Manaḥ ॥

न पश्यामो मुखे दंष्ट्रां न पाशं वा कराञ्जले ।उत्तमार्णमवेक्ष्यैव तथाप्युद्वेजिते मनः ॥

As in the case of Yama, the Lord of death visually we may not find, protruding teeth, nose, etc. Yet, the debtor's mind trembles at the very sight of the creditor.

Dāridryam – दारिद्रयम्‌– Poverty

53. *Śatrau Sāntvaṃ Pratīkāraḥ Sarvarogeṣu Bheṣajam |*
Mṛtyau Mṛtyuñjayadhyānaṃ Dāridrye Tu Na Kiṃ Cana ॥

शत्रौ सान्त्वं प्रतीकारः सर्वरोगेषु भेषजम्‌ ।
मृत्यौ मृत्युञ्जयध्यानं दारिद्रये तु न किं चन ॥

A person can peace the enemy also by pleasing him. For all the diseases, it is possible to find one or other medicine in the world. In order to live a long healthy life, Lord Shiva can be worshipped with Mrityunjay Mantra. But there is nothing in this world that could remove the poverty.

54. *Śaktiṃ Karoti Sañcāre Śītoṣṇe Marṣayatyapi |*
Dīpayatyudare Vahniṃ Dāridryaṃ Paramauṣadham ॥

शक्तिं करोति सञ्चारे शीतोष्णे मर्षयत्यपि । दीपयत्युदरे वह्निं दारिद्रयं परमौषधम्‌ ॥

On account of poverty a person is forced to roam from place to place. His body gets good energy. It enables him to withstand the cold and the heat. It increases the fire of digestion in the stomach. Hence, poverty helps the person to have good health, as a best medicine.

55. *Giraṃ Skhalantīṃ Mīlantīṃ Dṛṣṭiṃ Pādau Visaṃsthulau |*
Protsāhayati Yācñāyāṃ Rājājñeva Daridratā ॥

गिरं स्खलन्तीं मीलन्तीं दृष्टिं पादौ विसंस्थुलौ ।
प्रोत्साहयति याच्चायां राजाज्ञेव दरिद्रता ॥

Due to extreme poverty, the tongue of a poor man babbles and the words warble out. His eyes close on its own. The feet are rendered sore through continuous roaming. At that time that demon named poverty provokes him to beg also.

56. *Jīryanti Rājavidveṣā Jīryantyavihitānyapi |*
Ākiñcanyabalāḍhyānāmantato'śmāpi Jīryati ॥

जीर्यन्ति राजविद्वेषा जीर्यन्त्यविहितान्यपि ।
आकिञ्चन्यबलाढ्यानामन्ततोऽश्मापि जीर्यति ॥

A poor man will be able to digest the wrongs done to him by a king. Even if he indulges in crimes, those acts will also be digested. Ultimately, if he needs to eat stones due to extreme poverty even those will get digested.

57. *Nāsya Corā Na Piśunā Na Dāyādā Na Pārthivāḥ |*
Dainyaṃ Rājyādapi Jyāyo Yadi Tattvaṃ Prabudhyate ॥

नास्य चोरा न पिशुना न दायादा न पार्थिवाः ।
दैन्यं राज्यादपि ज्यायो यदि तत्त्वं प्रबुध्यते ॥

Due to poverty, there is no fear of thief, no tale bearers are traitors, or even rulers. Hence, one who understands this Brahmam, the God of Supreme truth will consider poverty even superior to a king.

Dhaninaḥ – धनिनः – Rich People

Shlokas 53 to 57 above talked about poverty and the poor. Now, in contrary, it starts talking about wealth and the rich.

58. *Prakāśayatyahankāraṃ Pravartayati Taskarān |*
Protsāhayati Dāyādāmllākṣmīḥ Kiṃ Cidupasthitā ॥

प्रकाशयत्यहङ्कारं प्रवर्तयति तस्करान् ।
प्रोत्साहयति दायादांल्लाक्ष्मीः किं चिदुपस्थिता ॥

The ego of a rich man would come out in the open on its own. That will impel the thieves to steal his wealth. His own relatives will become very happy and stake a claim and his wealth.

59. *Viḍambayanti Ye Nityaṃ Vidagdhān Dhanino Janāḥ |*
Ta Eva Tu Viḍambyante Śriyā Kiñcidupekṣitāḥ ||

विडम्बयन्ति ये नित्यं विदग्धान् धनिनो जनाः ।
त एव तु विडम्ब्यन्ते श्रिया किञ्चिदुपेक्षिताः ॥

The rich people puffed up with pride of their wealth always insult the poor. But the same people, in due course of time, deserted by Lakshmi, the Goddess of wealth, will be ridiculed by the poor.

60. *Prāmāṇyabuddhiḥ Stotreṣu Devatābuddhirātmani |*
Kīṭabuddhirmanuṣyeṣu Nūtanāyāḥ Śriyaḥ Phalam ||

प्रामाण्यबुद्धिः स्तोत्रेषु देवताबुद्धिरात्मनि ।
कीटबुद्धिर्मनुष्येषु नूतनायाः श्रियः फलम् ॥

People who suddenly become rich, develop certain qualities. Like when others praise with the qualities, which they do not possess, they start believing that they have those qualities and imagine that they are like Gods and treat others like dirt.

61. *Śṛṇvanta Eva Pṛcchanti Paśyanto'pi Na Jānate |*
Viḍambanāni Dhanikāḥ Stotrāṇītyeva Manvate ||

शृण्वन्त एव पृच्छन्ति पश्यन्तोऽपि न जानते ।
विडम्बनानि धनिकाः स्तोत्राणीत्येव मन्वते ॥

Rich people value in flattery by repeatedly listening to the same praise heaped on them. They are highly pretentious by seeking to ignore things though noticed by them. They take even the words of ridicule directed on them as words of praise.

62. *Āvṛtya Śrīmadenāndhānanyonyakṛtasaṃvidaḥ |*
Svairaṃ Hasanti+Pārśvasthā Bālonmattapiśācavat ||

आवृत्य श्रीमदेनान्धानन्योन्यकृतसंविदः ।
स्वैरं हसन्ति+पार्श्वस्था बालोन्मत्तपिशाचवत् ॥

Rich people, puffed up with the pride of wealth, are scoffed at by people, in the same way as children, insane or possessed persons are surrounded by people who ridicule them by exchanging the signs among themselves.

63. *Stotavyaiḥ Stūyante Nityam Sevanīyaiśca Sevyate |*
Na Bibheti Na Jihreti Tathāpi Dhaniko Janaḥ ||

स्तोतव्यैः स्तूयन्ते नित्यं सेवनीयैश्च सेव्यते ।
न बिभेति न जिह्रेति तथापि धनिको जनः ॥

A wealthy man, is worshipped by the elders, who are fit enough to be honoured by him. By that he is neither ashamed nor afraid of such actions. Normal people will be ashamed when elders salute them.

64. *Kṣaṇamātram Grahāveśo Yāmamātram Surāmadaḥ |*
Lakṣmīmadastu Mūrkhāṇāmādehamanuvartate ||

क्षणमात्रं ग्रहावेशो याममात्रं सुरामदः ।लक्ष्मीमदस्तु मूर्खाणामादेहमनुवर्तते ॥

When a person is possessed, it lasts for some time only. When a man is inebriated such a state of intoxication lasts only for some hours. But when a man becomes arrogant due to his wealth, such an arrogance, will lose till the last moment of his life.

65. *Śrīrmāsamardhamāsam Vā Ceṣṭitvā Vinivartate |*
Vikārastu Tadārabdho Nityam Laśunagandhavat ||

श्रीर्मासमर्धमासं वा चेष्टित्वा विनिवर्तते । विकारस्तु तदारब्धो नित्यं लशुनगन्धवत् ॥

The wealth attained by a man, may stay with him for half a month or full month. After, which it may disappear. But the conceit arising out of such wealth, will stay with lose him permanently, as the smell of a garlic lingers even after it is swallowed or removed from its place.

66. *Kaṇṭhe Madaḥ Kodravajo Hṛdi Tāmbūlajo Maḍaḥ |*
Lakṣmīmadastu Sarvāṅge Putradāramukheṣvapi ||

कंठे मदः कोद्रवजो हृदि ताम्बूलजो मदः ।

लक्ष्मीमदस्तु सर्वाङ्गे पुत्रदारमुखेष्वपि ॥

The taste of kudo millet grains will stay in the throat till it is digested. The taste of betel leaves extends up to the heart. But the taste arising out of the possession of wealth extends to the whole body of a man. Such an arrogance, will also be reflected on the faces of his wife and children.

67. *Yatrāsīdasti Vā Lakṣmīstatronmadaḥ Pravartatām |*
Kule'pyavataratyeṣa Kuṣṭhāpasmāravatkatham ॥

यत्रासीदस्ति वा लक्ष्मीस्तत्रोन्मदः प्रवर्तताम् ।
कुलेऽप्यवतरत्येष कुष्ठापस्मारवत्कथम् ॥

The wealth, whether a person had in the past or who currently has inebriation caused in the mind, due to that wealth, continuously afflicts his family like leprosy and epilepsy.

68. *Adhyāpayanti Śāstrāṇi Tṛṇīkurvanti Paṇḍitān |*
Vismārayanti Jātiṃ Svāṃ Varāṭāḥ Pañcaṣā Kare ॥

अध्यापयन्ति शास्त्राणि तृणीकुर्वन्ति पण्डितान् ।
विस्मारयन्ति जातिं स्वां वराटाः पञ्चषा करे ॥

Possession of even 5 or 6 coins (a small wealth) induces one to teach others on the finer points of shastras. Impels him to disregard even great scholars and makes him forget the honour of his caste and family.

All that one needs to be able to give lectures on every subject, not care a bit for the learned and forget one's past are a few pennies in the pocket.

69. *Bibhartu Bhṛtyān Dhaniko Dattāṃ Vā Deyamarthiṣu |*
Yāvadyācakasādharmyaṃ Tāvalloko Na Mṛṣyati ॥

बिभर्तु भृत्यान् धनिको दत्तां वा देयमर्थिषु ।
यावद्याचकसाधर्म्यं तावल्लोको न मृष्यति ॥

A wealthy man should help his servants and other needy people by generously giving money. Although the greed in him will restrain him from parting with his money, they expertise of the needy person will extract this money from him. Otherwise, his miserly quality will not allow the charity to take place.

Piśunāḥ – पिशुनाः – Lazy People

70. *Dhanabhāro Hi Lokasya Piśunaireva Dhāryate |*
Katham Te Tam Laghūkartum Yatante'parathā Svataḥ ||

धनभारो हि लोकस्य पिशुनैरेव धार्यते । कथं ते तं लघूकर्तुं यतन्तेऽपरथा स्वतः ॥

In this world, carrying the burden of a rich man's wealth is taken over by that tattle tale bearers. Otherwise, why should they come forward on their own to reduce the weight of that wealth. If a wealthy man is in the company of tattle tale bearers slowly his wealth will melt away.

71. *Śramānurūpam Piśune Kimupakriyate Nṛpaiḥ |*
Dviguṇam Triguṇam Caiva Kṛtānto Lālayiṣyati ||

श्रमानुरूपं पिशुने किमुपक्रियते नृपैः । द्विगुणं त्रिगुणं चैव कृतान्तो लालयिष्यति ॥

The kings do not sufficiently help that tale barrels in proportion to the troubles taken by them. On the contrary they are richly rewarded twice or thrice by Lord Yama, the Lord of death. Tale bearers will undergo sufferings at the hands of Lord Yama for the sins, they made.

72. *Gokarṇe Bhadrakarṇe Ca Japo Duṣkarmanāśanaḥ |*
Rājakarṇe Japaḥ Sadyaḥ Sarvakarmavināśanaḥ ||

गोकर्णे भद्रकर्णे च जपो दुष्कर्मनाशनः । राजकर्णे जपः सद्यः सर्वकर्मविनाशनः ॥

Even a little Japa, done in holy places such as Gokarna or Bhadra Karna will destroy all the sins done by a person. However, the tale telling in the ears of the king will instantly destroy all actions. Tales uttered by the tale bearers will miss lead the kings and lead them to take wrong decisions.

Note; The word *karṇam* in Samskrutam means ears.

73. *Na Svārthaṃ Kiñcidicchanti Na Preryante Ca Kena Cit |*
Parārtheṣu Pravartante Śaṭhāḥ Santaśca Tulyavat ||

न स्वार्थं किञ्चिदिच्छन्ति न प्रेर्यन्ते च केन चित् ।
परार्थेषु प्रवर्तन्ते शठाः सन्तश्च तुल्यवत् ॥

The good and the bad people are of the same type. The good people do not want anything for themselves. They do not do anything for their own and work selflessly. They also do not do anything just by other's prompting. They strive for the common good. Similarly bad people do not have any desire at all, in their belongings or properties. Wicked people also do not like their properties in the same way. They aim at stealing other's property without prompting. Thus, the focus of both good and bad people is centered on others.

74. *Kālāntare Hyanarthāya Gṛdhro Gehopari Sthitaḥ |*
Khalo Gṛhasamīpasthaḥ Sadyo'narthāya Dehinām ||

कालान्तरे ह्यनर्थाय गृध्रो गेहोपरि स्थितः ।
खलो गृहसमीपस्थः सद्योऽनर्थाय देहिनाम् ॥

It is generally believed that when eagles or vultures sit on the roof of the house, they will bring calamity to the householder after sometime. They are all considered as bad omen. However, if a bad person, resides near a good person's house, such a bad man instantaneously becomes the root cause of the householder's end.

Lobhinaḥ – लोभिनः – Greedy

75. *Śuṣkopavāso Dharmeṣu Bhaiṣajyeṣu Ca Laṅghanam |*
Japayajñaśca Yajñeṣu Rocate Lobhaśālinām ||

शुष्कोपवासो धर्मेषु भैषज्येषु च लङ्घनम् जपयज्ञश्च यज्ञेषु रोचते लोभशालिनाम् ॥

A greedy man, in order to hoard his wealth, will follow the fasting as set out in the Dharma Shastra as a best Dharma. Also, the cost of food is saved. Similarly, in case of illness, they would say it is better to starve among medicines. This is the cheapest medicine. Again of all the yagnas, the Japa Yagna, as it is the most inexpensive affairs, compared to conducting other religious rituals, which will lead to depletion of his wealth.

A miser likes these the most, since they are not expensive – Among religious observances, a complete fast, among treatment methods, postponement of a meal and among ways of worshipping god, chanting.

76. *Kiṃ Vakṣyatīva Dhanikādyāvadudvijate'dhanaḥ |*
Kiṃ Prakṣyatīti Lubdho'pi Tāvadudvijate Tataḥ ||

किं वक्ष्यतीव धनिकाद्यावदुद्विजतेऽधनः ।
किं प्रक्ष्यतीति लुब्धोऽपि तावदुद्विजते ततः ॥

A poor man when he sees a greedy rich man, will fear whether he would offer him any wealth or not. Whereas that greedy rich man will fear whether that poor man would beg from him any money.

77. *Sarvamātithyaśāstrārthaṃ Sākṣātkurvanti Lobhinaḥ |*
Bhikṣākabalamekaikaṃ Ye Hi Paśyanti Meruvat ||

सर्वमातिथ्यशास्त्रार्थं साक्षात्कुर्वन्ति लोभिनः ।
भिक्षाकबलमेकैकं ये हि पश्यन्ति मेरुवत् ॥

A greedy rich man considers each morsel of food offered to the guests, as if they are giving something equal and to Mount Meru. As per *Atithi Shastra* that a morsel of food, offered to a guest, is equivalent Mount Meru, that is that greedy rich man feels so.

78. *Dhanapālaḥ Piśāco Hi Datte Svāminyupasthite |*
Dhanalubdhaḥ Piśācastu Na Kasmai Cana Ditsate ||

धनपालः पिशाचो हि दत्ते स्वामिन्युपस्थिते ।
धनलुब्धः पिशाचस्तु न कस्मै चन दित्सते ॥

There are two types of ghosts, namely the ghost which guards the wealth and the ghost which is attached to the wealth. The first ghost will after be guarding the wealth will hand over the same to the owner. But the second ghost, which is attached to the wealth, will not part with that wealth to anyone.

These two ghosts can be compared to two types of people to whom wealth may be given for safeguarding. The first type will return the wealth. The second type due to the attachment and greediness to the wealth will not part with the same.

79. *Dātāro'rthibhirarthyante Dātṛbhiḥ Puno'rthinaḥ |*
Kartṛkarmavyatīhārādaho Nimnonnataṃ Kiyat ||

दातारोऽर्थिभिरर्थ्यन्ते दातृभिः पुनोऽर्थिनः ।
कर्तृकर्मव्यतीहारादहो निम्नोन्नतं कियत् ॥

Poor people beg from rich people. Later due to change in fortune, the same rich person may be reduced to poverty and may have to beg from the very same person whom they offered earlier. The giver become receiver and the receiver becomes giver. What a wonder is this in this era.

80. *Svasminnasati Nārthasya Rakṣakaḥ Sambhavediti |*
Niścityaivaṃ Svayamapi Bhuṅkte Lubdhaḥ Kathaṃ Cana ||

स्वस्मिन्नसति नार्थस्य रक्षकः सम्भवेदिति ।
निश्चित्यैवं स्वयमपि भुङ्क्ते लुब्धः कथं चन ॥

A miser believes that no one would take care of his wealth, after him. Hence, he protects it to the best extent possible. He even eats only as much minimum required to keep his breath in the body.

81. *Prasthāsyamānaḥ Praviśetpratiṣṭheta Dine Dine |*
Vicitrānullikhedvighnāṃstiṣṭhāsuratithiściram ||

प्रस्थास्यमानः प्रविशेत्प्रतिष्ठेत दिने दिने ।
विचित्रानुल्लिखेद्विघ्नां स्तिष्ठासुरतिथिश्चिरम् ॥

A miser guest who has come down to stay for a long period, will go away, if persuaded by some means by the householder. But he will again come back without being invited. Sometimes he will go back on his own and again come back. He will recount strange instances of obstacles that he faces in his travel.

Dhārmikāḥ – धार्मिकाः – Virtuous

82. Materials earning strategy

Ghaṭakaṃ Samyagārādhya Vairāgyaṃ Paramaṃ Vahet |
Tāvadarthāḥ Prasiddhyanti Yāvaccāpalamāvṛtam ||

घटकं सम्यगाराध्य वैराग्यं परमं वहेत् ।
तावदर्थाः प्रसिद्ध्यन्ति यावच्चापलमावृतम् ॥

A clever man, as long as he pretends with his benefactor that he is totally unattached to any material benefit, will learn enough money. Until he is exposed, he will continue to earn a lot of money.

83. *Ekataḥ Sarvaśāstrāṇi Tulasīkāṣṭhamekataḥ* |
Vaktavyaṃ Kiṃ Cidityuktaṃ Vastutastulasī Parā ||

एकतः सर्वशास्त्राणि तुलसीकाष्ठमेकतः ।
वक्तव्यं किं चिदित्युक्तं वस्तुतस्तुलसी परा ॥

A man with scholastic learning can earn money. There is another way of making money that is by wearing Holi Basil beeds – by becoming a dubious monk, a person may earn more money. As this is being recounted more later, only part of it is mentioned here.

84. *Vismṛtaṃ Vāhaṭenedaṃ Tulasyāḥ Paṭhatā Guṇan* |
Viśvasammohinī Vitta Dāyinīti Guṇadvayam ||

विस्मृतं वाहटेनेदं तुलस्याः पठता गुणन् विश्वसम्मोहिनी वित्त दायिनीति गुणद्वयम् ॥

Vāhaṭa, an expert on ancient medicines, who has spoken on the greatness of basil leaves, had forgotten to speak of its two important benefits. They are, it will delude the world and attract money.

Wearing Tulasi garland, a man can earn abundant wealth and mislead the world also.

85. Scumbags

Pradīyate Viduṣyekaṃ Kavau Daśa Naṭe Śatam |
Sahasraṃ Dāmbhike Loke Śrotriye Tu Na Kiñcana ||

प्रदीयते विदुष्येकं कवौ दश नटे शतम् । सहस्रं दाम्भिके लोके श्रोत्रिये तु न किञ्चन ॥

In this world, the money or gift given to a scholar will be 1%, to a poet 10%, to an actor 100% and to a Hoax 1,000%. But nothing will be given to a Vedic scholar. The Vedic scholar will not be able to earn enough money in this modern world.

86. *Kaupīnaṃ Bhasitālepo Darbhā+Rudrākṣamālikā |*
Maunamekāsikā Ceti Mūrkhasañjīvanāni Ṣaṭ ||

कौपीनं भसितालेपो दर्भा+रुद्राक्षमालिका ।
मौनमेकासिका चेति मूर्खसञ्जीवनानि षट् ॥

Wearing only a loin cloth, smearing holy ash all over the body, sitting on the seat of holy *Kucha* (*darba*) grass, wearing Rudraksha beads, keeping silent and sitting like a rock in a place, all these 6 are the means to make money for fools.

87. *Vāsaḥ Puṇyeṣu Tīrtheṣu Prasiddhaśca Mṛto Guruḥ |*
Adhyāpanāvṛttayaśca Kīrtanīyā Dhanārthibhiḥ ||

वासः पुण्येषु तीर्थेषुप्रसिद्धश्च मृतो गुरुः ।
अध्यापनावृत्तयश्च कीर्तनीया धनार्थिभिः ॥

People who want to make money should state that they come from very Holy towns, their Guru or teacher was a great Saint, who passed away long ago and they have lot many disciples. Making these assertions will make one eligible as an object of veneration. As a result, money will be showered on them.

88. *Mantrabhraṃśe Sampradāyaḥ Prayogaścyutasaṅkṛtau |*

Deśadharmastvanācāre Pṛcchatāṃ Siddhamuttaram ॥

मन्त्रभ्रंशे सम्प्रदायः प्रयोगश्च्युतसङ्कृतौ । देशधर्मस्त्वनाचारे पृच्छतां सिद्धमुत्तरम् ॥

If someone points out any mistake in the recitation of the mantras by a dubious or half-baked person, he should promptly reply that this was the method taught by his Guru. Similarly, he should say that if some samskaras are missed out, atonement is being done. If some unethical behavior occurs, he should immediately without even thinking it is the native custom where he hailed. It means that never a mistake has to be accepted and what he is doing is always correct.

89. *Yathā Jānanti Bahavo Yathā Vakṣyanti Dātari |*
Tathā Dharmaṃ Caretsarvaṃ Na Vṛthā Kiṃ Cidācaret ॥

यथा जानन्ति बहवो यथा वक्ष्यन्ति दातरि ।
तथा धर्मं चरेत्सर्वं न वृथा किं चिदाचरेत् ॥

Hypocrites do acts of charity pompously, in order to show off to the whole world. If no one takes notice of the same, they will not do any charity at all.

90. *Sadā Japapaṭo Haste Madhye Madhye'kṣimīlanam |*
Sarvaṃ Brahmeti Vādaśca Sadyaspratyayahetavaḥ ॥

सदा जपपटो हस्ते मध्ये मध्येऽक्षिमीलनम् । सर्वं ब्रह्मेति वादश्च सद्यस्प्रत्ययहेतवः ॥

Pretentious holy men always keep in hand rosery beads with a cloth to cover it and pretend to do penance. In between the recitation they close the eyes and frequently keep uttering that everything is Brahmam. These are all the ways to make people believe them.

91. *Āmadhyāhnaṃ Nadīvāsaḥ Samāje Devatārcanam |*
Satataṃ Śuciveśaśca Ityetaddambhasya Jīvitam ॥

आमध्याह्नं नदीवासः समाजे देवतार्चनम् ।
सततं शुचिवेषश्च इत्येतद्दम्भस्य जीवितम् ॥

परछिद्रेषु हृदयं परवार्तासु च श्रवः ।परमर्मासु वाचं च खलानामसृजद्विधिः ॥

Lord Brahma, the creator, has given the bad people, a mind to analyses the mistakes of others. ears to hear the secrets of others and tongue to speak ill or gossip about others.

The creator has placed the hearts of wicked men in others' defects, their ears in talks about others' and their speech in others' secrets.

99. *Viṣeṇa Pucchalagnena Vṛścikaḥ Prāṇināmiva |*
Kalinā Daśamāṃśena Sarvaḥ Kālo'pi Dāruṇaḥ ॥

विषेण पुच्छलग्नेन वृश्चिकः प्राणिनामिव ।
कलिना दशमांशेन सर्वः कालोऽपि दारुणः ॥

A scorpion terrorises other beings through the poison that has in its tail. The Kali Purusha or dark age of Kali, only through part of his rule (one tenth) over this earth has made this present age more terrifying than the bygone ages and to that extent worse than the scorpion.

100. *Yatra Bhāryāgiro Vedā Yatra Dharmo'rthasādhanam |*
Yatra Svapratibhā Mānaṃ Tasmai Śrīkalaye Namaḥ ॥

यत्र भार्यागिरो वेदा यत्र धर्मोऽर्थसाधनम् । यत्र स्वप्रतिभा मानं तस्मै श्रीकलये नमः ॥

In the age of Kali, where the words of one's wife are taken as the veritable code of contact or Dharma Shastra, where earning money is the only virtuous activity, where whatever thought appears in the mind is the Dharma or virtue, to that Kali Purush or dark age a big salutation.

101. *Kāmamastu Jagatsarvaṃ Kālasyāsya Vaśaṃvadam |*
Kālakālaṃ Prapannānāṃ Kālaḥ Kiṃ Naḥ Kariṣyati? ॥

काममस्तु जगत्सर्वं कालस्यास्य वशंवदम् ।
कालकालं प्रपन्नानां कालः किं नः करिष्यति? ॥

This whole world is being reigned by the dark age of Kali. But what can this age of Kali do to devout, who has totally surrendered himself to Lord Shankara, the one who determines the life of Yaman, the God of death? Nothing can be done by the Kali purusha to that devotee.

Even able ministers cannot save a kingdom that has no king. Strong winds cannot bring back to life a body bereft of its vital breath.

102.   *Kavinā Nīlakaṇṭhena Kaleretadviḍambanam |*
Racitaṃ Viduṣāṃ Prītyai Rājāsthānānumodanam ॥

कविना नीलकण्ठेन कलेरेतद्द्विडम्बनम् । रचितं विदुषां प्रीत्यै राजास्थानानुमोदनम् ॥

This satirical work by the name Kalividambana, has been composed by the poet Sri Neelakanta, for the purpose of regaling the intellectual giants decorating the court of a king.

*****

If the above satirical 102 stanzas can be summarized, about the behaviour of various types of people;

Ministers and Academics;
One should not be afraid, need not understand, nor even listen to the opposite side's arguments. One should reply immediately, if one desires to win in the assemblies.

Absence of flurry, setting no store by modesty, scorn of the opponent, laughter, eulogy of the king (the presiding judge), these five are the means of victory.

If the judge is not learned, win (your case) by shouting aloud; if he is learned, his line may be toed.

He who desires to know the truth should practice for long in modesty. But he who desires to win should throw away modesty and make a lot of noise.

Yogins and Sannyasis;

If our intellect cannot apply itself at all to any branch of knowledge, let us become practitioners of mantras, yogins, or even sannyasins.

If the thing succeeds without delay, the practitioners of mantras attain fame. If it takes time, many accessory rites could be announced and thereby money earned.

They indeed are fortunate, the Mantrikas, who's telling the happy ones that they will have happy and the unhappy ones that they will have a hard lot, itself becomes their blessings to them.

Silence due to ignorance, quaint conduct—all these would redound, in the case of the mantra-practitioner, to his greatness.

Astrologers;

Astrologers should make enquiries with messengers in the court and then predict results to the kings, for the movement of planets is necessary for them.

In questions regarding progeny, the astrologer should tell the father that it will be a son and the mother, a daughter, thereby he succeeds.

On queries about life, astrologers should say 'long life', if those who had consulted live on, they will honour the astrologer, if they die, whom could they ask?

Those who read the destiny (of people) should say that everything has two sides, everything is bound by good and bad periods and everything is a mixed bag.

By predicting wealth for the poor and more wealth for the rich, the astrologers, by all means, become popular and rich in this world.

Rich People;

Even the little affluence that comes uncovers one's pride, sets thieves on one and makes agnates busy.

The same rich people who mock at the learned, become themselves objects of mockery when dame fortune turns away even a little from them.

Believing flattery as true, considering oneself as a god, taking men to be worms—these are the fruits of new-found wealth.

Even as they are listening, the rich men will ask, even if they see, they do not know and if they are made fun of, they consider all that as praise!

The possession by spirits is momentary. The intoxication of liquor is for one *yaama* (three hours). But the pride of wealth of the fools continues till death.

Wealth does its antics for a month or a fortnight and goes away. But the changes it had given rise to, persist (in a person) forever, as the smell of a garlic.

The intoxication of Kodava is throat-deep, that of pan goes up to the heart, but that of wealth pervades the whole body and infects the mouths of the sons and wives of the rich.

Let there be intoxication where wealth had once been or is now present. But like leprosy and epilepsy it descends in the family!

Five or six pieces of coins in one's hand embolden one to teach texts, look down upon (other) scholars and make one forget one's class.

Lazy people;

Loin-cloth, smearing oneself with ash, sacred grass, rosary, silence, sitting all alone — these provide livelihood for stupid fellows, pretending to be monks.

The studious monks, who desire to get money should speak of their having stayed at sacred places, mention a well-known dead scholar as their teacher and the endowments which kings had made for their families to carry on teaching.

If somebody questions about deficiency in Mantras in what the pretending monks do, he says that that is the tradition (Sampradaya). If he is asked about the deficiency in the proper form of the sacrament, he would say that such is the practical way of doing it (*Prayoga*). if he is asked about lack of the prescribed conduct, he says that that is the way of people of his part of the country. These are the ready-made answers.

Always keeping the rosary and its covering cloth in hand, closing eyes every now and then, uttering "everything is Brahmam"—these produce confidence immediately.

Staying on at the river-side till noon, worshipping an image in public, always putting on the dress of purity — this is the secret of pretending sanyasis.

Religious acts should be prolonged only so long as there are onlookers. The moment there is none to witness, everything will to be closed.

Tears of joy and horripilation — If these two are at one's beck and call, what other religious acts does one require? Kings will become one's servant.

And finally, the author, Nīlakaṇṭha's parting shots are;

- One's wife's words are the scriptures,
- The only Dharma is to gather wealth,
- Just what strike's one is the authority,
- To that glorious Kali age be our obeisance!

Sarcastically lots of negative aspects of Kali Yuga have been detailed in this hymn. However, still lots of positive Dharma related activities do happen in this world especially in Sanatana Dharma of our Bharath. The negative aspects were stressed just to avoid those areas and be cautious. Let us follow the path of Dharma and lead a positive and happy life.

Iti Nīlakaṇṭhadīkṣitaviracitaṃ Kaliviḍambanaṃ Sampūrṇam |

इति नीलकण्ठदीक्षितविरचितं कलिविडम्बनं सम्पूर्णम् ।

KALI
YUGA

*****

Kaliviḍambana Stotram (Samskrutam)

कलिविडम्बनम्

न भेतव्यं न बोद्धव्यं न श्राव्यं वादिनो वचः ।
झटिति प्रतिवक्तव्यं सभासु विजिगीषुभिः ॥१

असम्भ्रमो विलज्जत्वमवज्ञा प्रतिवादिनि ।
हासो राज्ञः स्तवश्श्रेति पञ्चैते जयहेतवः ॥ २

उच्चैरुद्धोष्य जेतव्यं मध्यस्थश्चेदपण्डितः ।
पण्डितो यदि तत्रैव पक्षपातोऽधिरोप्यताम् ॥ ३

लोभो हेतुर्धनं साध्यं दृष्टान्तस्तु पुरोहितः ।
आत्मोत्कर्षो निगमनमनुमानेष्वयं विधिः ॥ ४

अभ्यास्यं लज्जमानेन तत्त्वं जिज्ञासुना चिरम् ।
जिगीषुना हियं त्यक्त्वा कार्यः कोलाहलो महान् ॥ ५

पाठनैर्ग्रन्थनिर्माणैः प्रतिष्ठा तावदाप्यते ।
एवं च तथ्यव्युत्पत्तिरायुषोऽन्ते भवेन्न वा ॥६

स्तोतारः के भविष्यन्ति मूर्खस्य जगतीतले ।
न स्तौति चेत्स्वयं च स्वं कदा तस्यास्तु निर्वृतिः ॥७

वाच्यतां समयोऽतीतः स्पष्टमग्रे भविष्यति ।
इति पाठयतां ग्रन्थे काठिन्यं कुत्र वर्तते ॥८

अगतित्वमतिश्रद्धा ज्ञानाभासेन तृप्तता ।
त्रयः शिष्यगुणा ह्येते मूर्खाचार्यस्य भाग्यजाः ॥९

यदि न क्वापि विद्यायां सर्वथा क्रमते मतिः ।
मान्त्रिकास्तु भविष्यामो योगिनो यतयोऽपि वा ॥ १०

अविलम्बेन संसिद्धौ मान्त्रिकैराप्यते यशः ।
विलम्बे कर्मबाहुल्यं विख्याप्यावाप्यते धनम् ॥ ११

सुखं सुखिषु दुःखेऽपि जीवनं दुःखशालिषु ।
अनुग्रहायते येषां ते धन्याः खलु मान्त्रिकाः ॥ १२

यावदज्ञानतो मौनमाचारो वा विलक्षणः ।
तावन्माहात्म्यरूपेण पर्यवस्यति मान्त्रिके अः ॥ १३

चारान् विचार्य दैवज्ञैर्वक्तव्यं भूभुजां फलम् ।
ग्रहचारपरिज्ञानं तेषामावश्यकं यतः ॥ १४

पुत्र इत्येव पितरि कन्यकेति मातरि ।
गर्भप्रश्नेषु कथयन् दैवज्ञो विजयी भवेत् ॥ १५

आयुःप्रश्ने दीर्घमायुर्वाच्यं मौहूर्तिकैर्जनैः ।
जीवन्तो बहुमन्यन्ते मृताः प्रक्ष्यन्ति कं पुनः ॥ १६

सर्वं कोटिद्वयोपेतं सर्वं कालद्वयावधि ।
सर्वं व्यामिश्रमिव च वक्तव्यं दैवचिन्तकैः ॥ १७

निर्धनानां धनावाप्तिं धनिनामधिकं धनम् ।
ब्रुवाणाः सर्वथा ग्राह्या लोकैज्ज्यौतिषिका जनाः ॥ १८

शतस्य लाभे ताम्बूलं सहस्रस्य तु भोजनम् ।
दैवज्ञानामुपालम्भो नित्यः कार्यविपर्यये ॥ १९

अपि सागरपर्यन्ता विचेतव्या वसुन्धरा ।
देशो ह्यरत्निमात्रेऽपि नास्ति दैवज्ञवर्जितः ॥ २०

वारान् के चिद्ग्रहान् के चित्के चिदृक्षाणि जानते ।
त्रितयं ये विजानन्ति ते वाचस्पतयः स्वयम् ॥ २१

नैमित्तिकाः स्वप्नदृशो देवतानां [[अमी त्रयः]] ।
निसर्गशत्रवः सृष्टा दैवज्ञानाममी त्रयः ॥ २२

स्वस्थैरसाध्यरोगैश्च जन्तुभिर्नास्ति किं चन ।
कातरा दीर्घरोगाश्च भिषजां भाग्यहेतवः ॥ २३

नातिधैर्यं प्रदातव्यं नातिभीतिश्च रोगिणि ।

नैश्चिन्त्यान्नादिमे दानं नैराश्यादेव नान्तिमे ॥ २४

भैषज्यं तु यथाकामं पथ्यं तु कठिनं वदेत् ।
आरोग्यं वैद्यमाहात्म्यादन्यथात्वमपथ्यतः ॥ २५

निदानं रोगनामानि सात्म्यासात्म्ये चिकित्सितम् ।
सर्वमप्युपदेक्ष्यन्ति रोगिणः सदने स्त्रियः ॥ २६

जृम्भमाणेषु रोगेषु म्रियमाणेषु जन्तुषु ।
रोगतत्त्वेषु शनकैर्व्युत्पद्यन्ते चिकित्सकाः ॥ २७

प्रवर्तनार्थमारम्भे मध्ये त्वौषधहेतवे ।
बहुमानार्थमन्ते च जिहीर्षन्ति चिकित्सकाः ॥ २८

लिप्समानेषु वैद्येषु चिरादासाद्य रोगिणम् ।
दायादाः सम्प्ररोहन्ति दैवज्ञा मान्त्रिका अपि ॥ २९

रोगस्योपक्रमे सान्त्वं मध्ये किं चिद्धनव्ययः ।
शनैरनादरस्शान्तौ स्नातो वैद्यं न पश्यति ॥ ३०

दैवज्ञत्वं मान्त्रिकता भैषज्यं चाटुकौशलम् ।
एकैकमर्थलाभाय द्वित्रियोगस्तु दुर्लभः ॥ ३१

अनृतं चाटुवादश्च धनयोगो महानयम् ।
सत्यं वैदुष्यमित्येष योगो दारिद्र्यकारकः ॥ ३२

कातर्यं दुर्विनीतत्त्वं कार्पण्यमविवेकताम् ।
सर्वं मार्जन्ति कवयः शालीनां मुष्टिकिङ्कराः ॥ ३३

न कारणमपेक्षन्ते कवयः स्तोतुमुद्यताः ।
किं चिदस्तुवतां तेषां जिह्वा फुरफुरायते ॥ ३४

स्तुतं स्तुवन्ति कवयो न स्वतो गुणदर्शिनः ।
कीतः कश्चिदलिर्नाम कियती तत्र वर्णना ॥ ३५

एकैव कविता पुंसां ग्रामायाश्वाय हस्तिने ।
अन्ततोऽन्नाय वस्त्राय ताम्बूलाय च कल्पते ॥ ३६

शब्दाख्यमपरं ब्रह्म सन्दर्भेण परिष्कृतम् ।
विक्रीयते कतिपयैर्वृथान्यैर्विनियुज्यते ॥ ३७

वर्णयन्ति नराभासान् वाणीं लब्ध्वापि ये जनाः ।
लब्ध्वापि कामधेनुं ते लाङ्गले विनियुञ्जते ॥ ३८

प्रशंसन्तो नराभासान् प्रलपन्तोऽन्यथान्यथा ।
कथं तरन्तु कवयः कामपारम्यवादिनः ॥ ३९

यत्सन्दर्भे यदुल्लेखे यद्व्यङ्ग्ये निभृतं मनः ।
समाधेरपि तज्ज्यायाः शङ्करो यदि वर्ण्यते ॥ ४०

बन्धवः :

गृहिणी भगिनी तस्याः श्वशुरौ श्याल इत्यपि ।
प्राणिनां कलिना सृष्टाः पञ्च प्राणा इमेऽपरे ॥ ४१

जामातरो भागिनेया मातुला दारबान्धवाः ।
अज्ञाता एव गृहिणां भक्ष्यन्त्याखुवद्गृहे ॥ ४२

मातुलस्य बलं माता जामातुर्दुहिता बलम् ।
श्वशुरस्य बलं भार्या स्वयमेवातिथेर्बलम् ॥ ४३

जामातुर्वक्रता तावद्यावच्छ्यालस्य बालता ।
प्रबुध्यमाने सारल्यं प्रबुद्धेऽस्मिन् पलायनम् ॥ ४४

भार्या ज्येष्ठा शिशुः श्यालः श्वश्रूः स्वातन्त्र्यवर्तिनी ।
श्वशुरस्तु प्रवासीति जामातुर्भाग्यधोरणी ॥ ४५

भूषणैर्वासनैः पात्रैः पुत्राणामुपलालनैः ।
सकृदागत्य गच्छन्ती कन्या निर्मार्ष्टि मन्दिरम् ॥ ४६

गृहिणी स्वजनं वक्ति शुष्काहारं मिताशनम् ।
पतिपक्ष्यांस्तु बह्वाशान् क्षीरपांस्तस्करानपि ॥ ४७

भार्ये द्वे पुत्रशालिन्यौ भगिनी पतिवर्जिता ।
अश्रान्तकलहो नाम योगोऽयं गृहमेधिनाम् ॥ ४८

भार्ये द्वे बहवः पुत्रा दारिद्र्यं रोगसम्भवः ।
जीर्णौ च मातापितरावेकैकं नरकाधिकम् ॥ ४९

उत्तमर्णाः

स्मृते सीदन्ति गात्राणि दृष्टे प्रज्ञा विनश्यति ।
अहो महदिदं भूतमुत्तमर्णाभिशाब्दितम् ॥ ५०

अन्तकोऽपि हि जन्तूनामन्तकालमपेक्षते ।
न कालनियमः कश्चिदुत्तमार्णस्य विद्यते ॥ ५१

न पश्यामो मुखे दंष्ट्रां न पाशं वा कराञ्जले ।
उत्तमार्णमवेक्ष्यैव तथाप्युद्वेजिते मनः ॥ ५२

दारिद्र्यम्

शत्रौ सान्त्वं प्रतीकारः सर्वरोगेषु भेषजम् ।
मृत्यौ मृत्युञ्जयध्यानं दारिद्र्ये तु न किं चन ॥ ५३

शक्तिं करोति सञ्चारे शीतोष्णे मर्षयत्यपि ।
दीपयत्युदरे वह्निं दारिद्र्यं परमौषधम् ॥ ५४

गिरं स्खलन्तीं मीलन्तीं दृष्टिं पादौ विसंस्थुलौ ।
प्रोत्साहयति याच्ञायां राजाज्ञेव दरिद्रता ॥ ५५

जीर्यन्ति राजविद्वेषा जीर्यन्त्यविहितान्यपि ।
आकिञ्चन्यबलाढ्यानामन्ततोऽश्मापि जीर्यति ॥ ५६

नास्य चोरा न पिशुना न दायादा न पार्थिवाः ।
दैन्यं राज्यादपि ज्यायो यदि तत्त्वं प्रबुध्यते ॥ ५७

धनिनः

प्रकाशयत्यहङ्कारं प्रवर्तयति तस्करान् ।
प्रोत्साहयति दायादांल्लक्ष्मीः किं चिदुपस्थिता ॥ ५८

विडम्बयन्ति ये नित्यं विदग्धान् धनिनो जनाः ।
त एव तु विडम्ब्यन्ते श्रिया किञ्चिदुपेक्षिताः ॥ ५९

प्रामाण्यबुद्धिः स्तोत्रेषु देवताबुद्धिरात्मनि ।
कीटबुद्धिर्मनुष्येषु नूतनायाः श्रियः फलम् ॥ ६०

शृण्वन्त एव पृच्छन्ति पश्यन्तोऽपि न जानते ।
विडम्बनानि धनिकाः स्तोत्राणीत्येव मन्वते ॥ ६१

आवृत्य श्रीमदेनान्धानन्योन्यकृतसंविदः ।
स्वैरं हसन्ति+पार्श्वस्था बालोन्मत्तपिशाचवत् ॥ ६२

स्तोतव्यैः स्तूयन्ते नित्यं सेवनीयैश्च सेव्यते ।
न बिभेति न जिह्रेति तथापि धनिको जनः ॥ ६३

क्षणमात्रं ग्रहावेशो याममात्रं सुरामदः ।
लक्ष्मीमदस्तु मूर्खाणामादेहमनुवर्तते ॥ ६४

श्रीमासमर्धमासं वा चेष्टित्वा विनिवर्तते ।
विकारस्तु तदारब्धो नित्यं लशुनगन्धवत् ॥ ६५

कंठे मदः कोद्रवजो हृदि ताम्बूलजो मदः ।
लक्ष्मीमदस्तु सर्वाङ्गे पुत्रदारमुखेष्वपि ॥ ६६

यत्रासीदस्ति वा लक्ष्मीस्तत्रोन्मदः प्रवर्तताम् ।
कुलेऽप्यवतरत्येष कुष्ठापस्मारवत्कथम् ॥ ६७

अध्यापयन्ति शास्त्राणि तृणीकुर्वन्ति पण्डितान् ।
विस्मारयन्ति जातिं स्वां वराटाः पञ्चषा करे ॥ ६८

बिभर्तु भृत्यान् धनिकोदत्तां वा देयमर्थिषु ।
यावद्याचकसाधर्म्यं तावल्लोको न मृष्यति ॥ ६९

पिशुनाः

धनभारो हि लोकस्य पिशुनैरेव धार्यते ।
कथं ते तं लघूकर्तुं यतन्तेऽपरथा स्वतः ॥ ७०

श्रमानुरूपं पिशुने किमुपक्रियते नृपैः ।
द्विगुणं त्रिगुणं चैव कृतान्तो लालयिष्यति ॥ ७१

गोकर्णे भद्रकर्णे च जपो दुष्कर्मनाशनः ।
राजकर्णे जपः सद्यः सर्वकर्मविनाशनः ॥ ७२

न स्वार्थं किञ्चिदिच्छन्ति न प्रेर्यन्ते च केन चित् ।
परार्थेषु प्रवर्तन्ते शठाः सन्तश्च तुल्यवत् ॥ ७३

कालान्तरे ह्यनर्थाय गृध्रो गेहोपरि स्थितः ।
खलो गृहसमीपस्थः सद्योऽनर्थाय देहिनाम् ॥ ७४

लोभिनः

शुष्कोपवासो धर्मेषु भैषज्येषु च लङ्घनम् ।
जपयज्ञश्च यज्ञेषु रोचते लोभशालिनाम् ॥ ७५

किं वक्ष्यतीव धनिकाद्यावद्विजतेऽधनः ।
किं प्रक्ष्यतीति लुब्धोऽपि तावद्विजते ततः ॥ ७६

सर्वमातिथ्यशास्त्रार्थं साक्षात्कुर्वन्ति लोभिनः ।
भिक्षाकबलमेकैकं ये हि पश्यन्ति मेरुवत् ॥ ७७

धनपालः पिशाचो हि दत्ते स्वामिन्युपस्थिते ।
धनलुब्धः पिशाचस्तु न कस्मै चन दित्सते ॥ ७८

दातारोऽर्थिभिरर्थ्यन्ते दातृभिः पुनोऽर्थिनः ।
कर्तृकर्मव्यतीहारादहो निम्नोन्नतं कियत् ॥ ७९

स्वस्मिन्नसति नार्थस्य रक्षकः सम्भवेदिति ।
निश्चित्यैवं स्वयमपि भुङ्क्ते लुब्धः कथं चन ॥ ८०

प्रस्थास्यमानः प्रविशेत्प्रतिष्ठेत दिने दिने ।
विचित्रानुल्लिखेद्द्विघ्नां स्तिष्ठासुरतिथिश्चिरम् ॥ ८१

धार्मिकाः

प्रदीयते विदुष्येकं कवौ दश नटे शतम् ।
सहस्रं दाम्भिके लोके श्रोत्रिये तु न किञ्चन ॥ ८२

घटकं सम्यगाराध्य वैराग्यं परमं वहेत् ।
तावदर्थाः प्रसिद्ध्यन्ति यावच्चापलमावृतम् ॥ ८३

एकतः सर्वशास्त्राणि तुलसीकाष्ठमेकतः ।
वक्तव्यं किं चिदित्युक्तं वस्तुतस्तुलसी परा ॥ ८४

विस्मृतं वाहटेनेदं तुलस्याः पठता गुणन् ।
विश्वसम्मोहिनी वित्त दायिनीति गुणद्वयम् ॥ ८५

कौपीनं भसितालेपो दर्भा+रुद्राक्षमालिका ।
मौनमेकासिका चेति मूर्खसञ्जीवनानि षट् ॥ ८६

वासः पुण्येषु तीर्थेषु प्रसिद्धश्च मृतो गुरुः ।
अध्यापनावृत्तयश्च कीर्तनीया धनार्थिभिः ॥ ८७

मन्त्रभ्रंशे सम्प्रदायः प्रयोगश्च्युतसङ्कृतौ ।
देशधर्मस्त्वनाचारे पृच्छतां सिद्धमुत्तरम् ॥ ८८

यथा जानन्ति बहवो यथा वक्ष्यन्ति दातरि ।
तथा धर्मं चरेत्सर्वं न वृथा किं चिदाचरेत् ॥ ८९

सदा जपपटो हस्ते मध्ये मध्येऽक्षिमीलनम् ।
सर्वं ब्रह्मेति वादश्च सद्यःप्रत्ययहेतवः ॥ ९०

आमध्याह्नं नदीवासः समाजे देवतार्चनम् ।
सततं शुचिवेषश्च इत्येतद्दम्भस्य जीवितम् ॥ ९१

तावद्दीर्घं नित्यकर्म यावत्स्याद्द्रष्टृमेलनम् ।
तावत्सङ्क्षिप्यते सर्वं यावद्द्रष्टा न विद्यते ॥ ९२

आनन्दबाष्परोमाञ्चौ यस्य स्वेच्छावशंवदौ ।
किं तस्य साधनैरन्यैः किङ्कराः सर्वपार्थिवाः ॥ ९३

दुर्जनाः

दण्ड्यमाना विकुर्वन्ति लाल्यमानास्ततस्तराम् ।
दुर्जनानामतो न्याय्यं दूरादेव विसर्जनम् ॥ ९४

अदानमीषद्दानं च किञ्चित्कोपाय दुर्धियाम् ।
सम्पूर्णदानं प्रकृतिर्विरामो वैरकारणम् ॥ ९५

ज्यायानसंस्तवो दुष्टैरीर्ष्यायै संस्तवः पुनः ।
अपत्यसम्बन्धविधिः स्वानर्थायैव केवलम् ॥ ९६

ज्ञातेयं ज्ञानहीनत्वं पिशुनत्वं दरिद्रता ।
मिलन्ति यदि चत्वारि तद्विशेऽपि नमो नमः ॥ ९७

परच्छिद्रेषु हृदयं परवार्तासु च श्रवः ।
परमर्मासु वाचं च खलानामसृजद्विधिः ॥ ९८

विषेण पुच्छलग्नेन वृश्चिकः प्राणिनामिव ।
कलिना दशमांशेन सर्वः कालोऽपि दारुणः ॥ ९९

यत्र भार्यागिरो वेदा यत्र धर्मोऽर्थसाधनम् ।
यत्र स्वप्रतिभा मानं तस्मै श्रीकलये नमः ॥ १००

काममस्तु जगत्सर्वं कालस्यास्य वशंवदम् ।
कालकालं प्रपन्नानां कालः किं नः करिष्यति? ॥ १०१

कविना नीलकण्ठेन कलेरेतद्विडम्बनम् ।
रचितं विदुषां प्रीत्यै राजास्थानानुमोदनम्। १०२

इति नीलकण्ठदीक्षितविरचितं
कलिविडम्बनं सम्पूर्णम् ।

*****

Kaliviḍambana Stotram (English)

Na Bhetavyaṃ Na Boddhavyaṃ Na Śrāvyaṃ Vādino Vacaḥ |
Jhaṭiti Prativaktavyaṃ Sabhāsu Vijigīṣubhiḥ ‖ 1

Asambhramo Vilajjatvamavajñā Prativādini |
Hāso Rājñaḥ Stavaśceti Pañcaite Jayahetavaḥ ‖ 2

Uccairudghoṣya Jetavyaṃ Madhyasthaścedapaṇḍitaḥ |
Paṇḍito Yadi Tatraiva Pakṣapāto'dhiropyatām ‖ 3

Lobho Heturdhanaṃ Sādhyaṃ Dṛṣṭāntastu Purohitaḥ |
Ātmotkarṣo Nigamanamanumāneṣvayaṃ Vidhiḥ ‖ 4

Abhyāsyaṃ Lajjamānena Tattvaṃ Jijñāsunā Ciram |
Jigīṣunā Hriyaṃ Tyaktvā Kāryaḥ Kolāhalo Mahān ‖ 5

Pāṭhanairgranthanirmāṇaiḥ Pratiṣṭhā Tāvadāpyate |
Evaṃ Ca Tathyavyutpattirāyuṣo'nte Bhavenna Vā ‖ 6

Stotāraḥ Ke Bhaviṣyanti Mūrkhasya Jagatītale |
Na Stauti Cetsvayaṃ Ca Svaṃ Kadā Tasyāstu Nirvṛtiḥ ‖ 7

Vācyatāṃ Samayo'tītaḥ Spaṣṭamagre Bhaviṣyati |
Iti Pāṭhayatāṃ Granthe Kāṭhinyaṃ Kutra Vartate ‖ 8

Agatitvamatiśraddhā Jñānābhāsena Tṛptatā |
Trayaḥ Śiṣyaguṇā Hyete Mūrkhācāryasya Bhāgyajāḥ ‖ 9

Yadi Na Kvāpi Vidyāyāṃ Sarvathā Kramate Matiḥ |
Māntrikāstu Bhaviṣyāmo Yogino Yatayo'pi Vā ‖ 10

Avilambena Saṃsiddhau Māntrikairāpyate Yaśaḥ |
Vilambe Karmabāhulyaṃ Vikhyāpyāvāpyate Dhanam ‖ 11

Sukhaṃ Sukhiṣu Duḥkhe'pi Jīvanaṃ Duḥkhaśāliṣu |

Anugrahāyate Yeṣāṃ Te Dhanyāḥ Khalu Māntrikāḥ ‖ 12

Yāvadajñānato Maunamācāro Vā Vilakṣaṇaḥ |

Tāvanmāhātmyarūpeṇa Paryavasyati Māntrike Aḥ ‖ 13

Cārān Vicārya Daivajñairvaktavyaṃ Bhūbhujāṃ Phalam |

Grahacāraparijñānaṃ Teṣāmāvaśyakaṃ Yataḥ ‖ 14

Putra Ityeva Pitari Kanyaketi Mātari |

Garbhapraśneṣu Kathayan Daivajño Vijayī Bhavet ‖ 15

Āyuspraśne Dīrghamāyurvācyaṃ Mauhūrtikairjanaiḥ |

Jīvanto Bahumanyante Mṛtāḥ Prakṣyanti Kaṃ Punaḥ ‖ 16

Sarvaṃ Koṭidvayopetaṃ Sarvaṃ Kāladvayāvadhi |

Sarvaṃ Vyāmiśramiva Ca Vaktavyaṃ Daivacintakaiḥ ‖ 17

Nirdhanānāṃ Dhanāvāptiṃ Dhanināmadhikaṃ Dhanam |

Bruvāṇāḥ Sarvathā Grāhyā Lokairjyautiṣikā Janāḥ ‖ 18

Śatasya Lābhe Tāmbūlaṃ Sahasrasya Tu Bhojanam |

Daivajñānāmupālambho Nityaḥ Kāryaviparyaye ‖ 19

Api Sāgaraparyantā Vicetavyā Vasundharā |

Deśo Hyaratnimātre'pi Nāsti Daivajñavarjitaḥ ‖ 20

Vārān Ke Cidgrahān Ke Citke Cidṛkṣāṇi Jānate |

Tritayaṃ Ye Vijānanti Te Vācaspatayaḥ Svayam ‖ 21

Naimittikāḥ Svapnadṛśo Devatānāṃ [[Amī Trayaḥ]] |

Nisargaśatravaḥ Sṛṣṭā Daivajñānāmamī Trayaḥ ‖ 22

Svasthairasādhyarogaiśca Jantubhirnāsti Kiṃ Cana |

Kātarā Dīrgharogāśca Bhiṣajāṃ Bhāgyahetavaḥ || 23

Nātidhairyaṃ Pradātavyaṃ Nātibhītiśca Rogiṇi |
Naiścintyānnādime Dānaṃ Nairāśyādeva Nāntime || 24

Bhaiṣajyaṃ Tu Yathākāmaṃ Pathyaṃ Tu Kaṭhinaṃ Vadet |
Ārogyaṃ Vaidyamāhātmyādanyathātvamapathyataḥ || 25

Nidānaṃ Roganāmāni Sātmyāsātmye Cikitsitam |
Sarvamapyupadekṣyanti Rogiṇaḥ Sadane Striyaḥ || 26

Jṛmbhamāṇeṣu Rogeṣu Mriyamāṇeṣu Jantuṣu |
Rogatattveṣu Śanakairvyutpadyante Cikitsakāḥ || 27

Pravartanārthamārambhe Madhye Tvauṣadhahetave |
Bahumānārthamante Ca Jihīrṣanti Cikitsakāḥ || 28

Lipsamāneṣu Vaidyeṣu Cirādāsādya Rogiṇam |
Dāyādāḥ Samprarohanti Daivajñā Māntrikā Api || 29

Rogasyopakrame Sāntvaṃ Madhye Kiṃ Ciddhanavyayaḥ |
Śanairanādarassāntau Snāto Vaidyaṃ Na Paśyati || 30

Daivajñatvaṃ Māntrikatā Bhaiṣajyaṃ Cāṭukauśalam |
Ekaikamarthalābhāya Dvitriyogastu Durlabhaḥ || 31

Anṛtaṃ Cāṭuvādaśca Dhanayogo Mahānayam |
Satyaṃ Vaiduṣyamityeṣa Yogo Dāridryakārakaḥ || 32

Kātaryaṃ Durvinītattvaṃ Kārpaṇyamavivekatām |
Sarvaṃ Mārjanti Kavayaḥ Śālīnāṃ Muṣṭikiṅkarāḥ || 33

Na Kāraṇamapekṣante Kavayaḥ Stotumudyatāḥ |
Kiṃ Cidastuvatāṃ Teṣāṃ Jihvā Phuraphurāyate || 34

Stutaṃ Stuvanti Kavayo Na Svato Guṇadarśinaḥ |

Kītaḥ Kaścidalirnāma Kiyatī Tatra Varṇanā || 35

Ekaiva Kavitā Puṃsāṃ Grāmāyāśvāya Hastine |

Antato'nnāya Vastrāya Tāmbūlāya Ca Kalpate || 36

Śabdākhyamaparaṃ Brahma Sandarbheṇa Pariṣkṛtam |

Vikrīyate Katipayairvṛthānyairviniyujyate || 37

Varṇayanti Narābhāsān Vāṇīṃ Labdhvāpi Ye Janāḥ |

Labdhvāpi Kāmadhenuṃ Te Lāṅgale Viniyuñjate || 38

Praśaṃsanto Narābhāsān Pralapanto'nyathānyathā |

Kathaṃ Tarantu Kavayaḥ Kāmapāramyavādinaḥ || 39

Yatsandarbhe Yadullekhe Yadvyaṅgye Nibhṛtaṃ Manaḥ |

Samādherapi Tajjyāyāḥ Śaṅkaro Yadi Varṇyate || 40

Bandhavaḥ

Gṛhiṇī Bhaginī Tasyāḥ Śvaśurau Śyāla Ityapi |

Prāṇināṃ Kalinā Sṛṣṭāḥ Pañca Prāṇā Ime'pare || 41

Jāmātaro Bhāgineyā Mātulā Dārabāndhavāḥ |

Ajñātā Eva Gṛhiṇāṃ Bhakṣyantyākhuvadgṛhe || 42

Mātulasya Balaṃ Mātā Jāmāturduhitā Balam |

Śvaśurasya Balaṃ Bhāryā Svayamevātitherbalam || 43

Jāmāturvakratā Tāvadyāvacchyālasya Bālatā |

Prabudhyamāne Sāralyaṃ Prabuddhe'smin Palāyanam || 44

Bhāryā Jyeṣṭhā Śiśuḥ Śyālaḥ Śvaśrūḥ Svātantryavartinī |

Śvaśurastu Pravāsīti Jāmāturbhāgyadhoraṇī || 45

Bhūṣaṇairvāsanaiḥ Pātraiḥ Putrāṇāmupalālanaiḥ |

Sakṛdāgatya Gacchantī Kanyā Nirmārṣṭi Mandiram ‖ 46

Gṛhiṇī Svajanaṃ Vakti Śuṣkāhāraṃ Mitāśanam |

Patipakṣyāṃstu Bahvāśān Kṣīrapāṃstaskarānapi ‖ 47

Bhārye Dve Putraśālinyau Bhaginī Pativarjitā |

Aśrāntakalaho Nāma Yogo'yaṃ Gṛhamedhinām ‖ 48

Bhārye Dve Bahavaḥ Putrā Dāridryaṃ Rogasambhavaḥ |

Jīrṇau Ca Mātāpitarāvekaikaṃ Narakādhikam ‖ 49

Uttamarṇāḥ

Smṛte Sīdanti Gātrāṇi Dṛṣṭe Prajñā Vinaśyati |

Aho Mahadidaṃ Bhūtamuttamarṇābhiśābdhitam ‖ 50

Antako'pi Hi Jantūnāmantakālamapekṣate |

Na Kālaniyamaḥ Kaściduttamārṇasya Vidyate ‖ 51

Na Paśyāmo Mukhe Daṃṣṭrāṃ Na Pāśaṃ Vā Karāñjale |

Uttamārṇamavekṣyaiva Tathāpyudvejite Manaḥ ‖ 52

Dāridryam

Śatrau Sāntvaṃ Pratīkāraḥ Sarvarogeṣu Bheṣajam |

Mṛtyau Mṛtyuñjayadhyānaṃ Dāridrye Tu Na Kiṃ Cana ‖ 53

Śaktiṃ Karoti Sañcāre Śītoṣṇe Marṣayatyapi |

Dīpayatyudare Vahniṃ Dāridryaṃ Paramauṣadham ‖ 54

Giraṃ Skhalantīṃ Mīlantīṃ Dṛṣṭiṃ Pādau Visaṃsthulau |

Protsāhayati Yācñāyāṃ Rājājñeva Daridratā ‖ 55

Jīryanti Rājavidveṣā Jīryantyavihitānyapi |

Ākiñcanyabalāḍhyānāmantato'śmāpi Jīryati || 56

Nāsya Corā Na Piśunā Na Dāyādā Na Pārthivāḥ |
Dainyaṃ Rājyādapi Jyāyo Yadi Tattvaṃ Prabudhyate || 57

Dhaninaḥ

Prakāśayatyahaṅkāraṃ Pravartayati Taskarān |
Protsāhayati Dāyādāṃllākṣmīḥ Kiṃ Cidupasthitā || 58

Viḍambayanti Ye Nityaṃ Vidagdhān Dhanino Janāḥ |
Ta Eva Tu Viḍambyante Śriyā Kiñcidupekṣitāḥ || 59

Prāmāṇyabuddhiḥ Stotreṣu Devatābuddhirātmani |
Kīṭabuddhirmanuṣyeṣu Nūtanāyāḥ Śriyaḥ Phalam || 60

Śṛṇvanta Eva Pṛcchanti Paśyanto'pi Na Jānate |
Viḍambanāni Dhanikāḥ Stotrāṇītyeva Manvate || 61

Āvṛtya Śrīmadenāndhānanyonyakṛtasaṃvidaḥ |
Svairaṃ Hasanti+Pārśvasthā Bālonmattapiśācavat || 62

Stotavyaiḥ Stūyante Nityaṃ Sevanīyaiśca Sevyate |
Na Bibheti Na Jihreti Tathāpi Dhaniko Janaḥ || 63

Kṣaṇamātraṃ Grahāveśo Yāmamātraṃ Surāmadaḥ |
Lakṣmīmadastu Mūrkhāṇāmādehamanuvartate || 64

Śrīrmāsamardhamāsaṃ Vā Ceṣṭitvā Vinivartate |
Vikārastu Tadārabdho Nityaṃ Laśunagandhavat || 65

Kaṇṭhe Madaḥ Kodravajo Hṛdi Tāmbūlajo Madaḥ |
Lakṣmīmadastu Sarvāṅge Putradāramukheṣvapi || 66

Yatrāsīdasti Vā Lakṣmīstatronmadaḥ Pravartatām |

Kule'pyavataratyeṣa Kuṣṭhāpasmāravatkatham || 67

Adhyāpayanti Śāstrāṇi Tṛṇīkurvanti Paṇḍitān |
Vismārayanti Jātiṃ Svāṃ Varāṭāḥ Pañcaṣā Kare || 68

Bibhartu Bhṛtyān Dhaniko Dattāṃ Vā Deyamarthiṣu |
Yāvadyācakasādharmyaṃ Tāvalloko Na Mṛṣyati || 69

Piśunāḥ

Dhanabhāro Hi Lokasya Piśunaireva Dhāryate |
Kathaṃ Te Taṃ Laghūkartuṃ Yatante'parathā Svataḥ || 70

Śramānurūpaṃ Piśune Kimupakriyate Nṛpaiḥ |
Dviguṇaṃ Triguṇaṃ Caiva Kṛtānto Lālayiṣyati || 71

Gokarṇe Bhadrakarṇe Ca Japo Duṣkarmanāśanaḥ |
Rājakarṇe Japaḥ Sadyaḥ Sarvakarmavināśanaḥ || 72

Na Svārthaṃ Kiñcidicchanti Na Preryante Ca Kena Cit |
Parārtheṣu Pravartante Śaṭhāḥ Santaśca Tulyavat || 73

Kālāntare Hyanarthāya Gṛdhro Gehopari Sthitaḥ |
Khalo Gṛhasamīpasthaḥ Sadyo'narthāya Dehinām || 74

Lobhinaḥ

Śuṣkopavāso Dharmeṣu Bhaiṣajyeṣu Ca Laṅghanam |
Japayajñaśca Yajñeṣu Rocate Lobhaśālinām || 75

Kiṃ Vakṣyatīva Dhanikādyāvadudvijate'dhanaḥ |
Kiṃ Prakṣyatīti Lubdho'pi Tāvadudvijate Tataḥ || 76

Sarvamātithyaśāstrārthaṃ Sākṣātkurvanti Lobhinaḥ |
Bhikṣākabalamekaikaṃ Ye Hi Paśyanti Meruvat || 77

Dhanapālaḥ Piśāco Hi Datte Svāminyupasthite |

Dhanalubdhaḥ Piśācastu Na Kasmai Cana Ditsate || 78

Dātāro'rthibhirarthyante Dātṛbhiḥ Puno'rthinaḥ |

Kartṛkarmavyatīhārādaho Nimnonnataṃ Kiyat || 79

Svasminnasati Nārthasya Rakṣakaḥ Sambhavediti |

Niścityaivaṃ Svayamapi Bhuṅkte Lubdhaḥ Kathaṃ Cana || 80

Prasthāsyamānaḥ Praviśetpratiṣṭheta Dine Dine |

Vicitrānullikhedvighnāṃstiṣṭhāsuratithiściram || 81

Dhārmikāḥ

Pradīyate Viduṣyekaṃ Kavau Daśa Naṭe Śatam |

Sahasraṃ Dāmbhike Loke Śrotriye Tu Na Kiñcana || 82

Ghaṭakaṃ Samyagārādhya Vairāgyaṃ Paramaṃ Vahet |

Tāvadarthāḥ Prasiddhyanti Yāvaccāpalamāvṛtam || 83

Ekataḥ Sarvaśāstrāṇi Tulasīkāṣṭhamekataḥ |

Vaktavyaṃ Kiṃ Cidityuktaṃ Vastutastulasī Parā || 84

Vismṛtaṃ Vāhaṭenedaṃ Tulasyāḥ Paṭhatā Guṇan |

Viśvasammohinī Vitta Dāyinīti Guṇadvayam || 85

Kaupīnaṃ Bhasitālepo Darbhā+Rudrākṣamālikā |

Maunamekāsikā Ceti Mūrkhasañjīvanāni Ṣaṭ || 86

Vāsaḥ Puṇyeṣu Tīrtheṣu Prasiddhaśca Mṛto Guruḥ |

Adhyāpanāvṛttayaśca Kīrtanīyā Dhanārthibhiḥ || 87

Mantrabhraṃśe Sampradāyaḥ Prayogaścyutasaṅkṛtau |

Deśadharmastvanācāre Pṛcchatāṃ Siddhamuttaram || 88

Yathā Jānanti Bahavo Yathā Vakṣyanti Dātari |

Tathā Dharmaṃ Caretsarvaṃ Na Vṛthā Kiṃ Cidācaret || 89

Sadā Japapaṭo Haste Madhye Madhye'kṣimīlanam |

Sarvaṃ Brahmeti Vādaśca Sadyaspratyayahetavaḥ || 90

Āmadhyāhnaṃ Nadīvāsaḥ Samāje Devatārcanam |

Satataṃ Śuciveṣaśca Ityetaddambhasya Jīvitam || 91

Tāvaddīrghaṃ Nityakarma Yāvatsyāddraṣṭṛmelanam |

Tāvatsaṅkṣipyate Sarvaṃ Yāvaddraṣṭā Na Vidyate || 92

Ānandabāṣparomāñcau Yasya Svecchāvaśaṃvadau |

Kiṃ Tasya Sādhanairanyaiḥ Kiṅkarāḥ Sarvapārthivāḥ || 93

Durjanāḥ

Daṇḍyamānā Vikurvanti Lālyamānāstatastarām |

Durjanānāmato Nyāyyaṃ Dūrādeva Visarjanam || 94

Adānamīṣaddānaṃ Ca Kiñcitkopāya Durdhiyām |

Sampūrṇadānaṃ Prakṛtirvirāmo Vairakāraṇam || 95

Jyāyānasaṃstavo Duṣṭairīrṣyāyai Saṃstavaḥ Punaḥ |

Apatyasambandhavidhiḥ Svānarthāyaiva Kevalam || 96

Jñāteyaṃ Jñānahīnatvaṃ Piśunatvaṃ Daridratā |

Milanti Yadi Catvāri Taddiśe'pi Namo Namaḥ || 97

Parachidreṣu Hṛdayaṃ Paravārtāsu Ca Śravaḥ |

Paramarmāsu Vācaṃ Ca Khalānāmasṛjadvidhiḥ || 98

Viṣeṇa Pucchalagnena Vṛścikaḥ Prāṇināmiva |

Kalinā Daśamāṃśena Sarvaḥ Kālo'pi Dāruṇaḥ || 99

Yatra Bhāryāgiro Vedā Yatra Dharmo'rthasādhanam |

Yatra Svapratibhā Mānaṃ Tasmai Śrīkalaye Namaḥ || 100

Kāmamastu Jagatsarvaṃ Kālasyāsya Vaśaṃvadam |

Kālakālaṃ Prapannānāṃ Kālaḥ Kiṃ Naḥ Kariṣyati? || 101

Kavinā Nīlakaṇṭhena Kaleretadviḍambanam |

Racitaṃ Viduṣāṃ Prītyai Rājāsthānānumodanam || 102

Iti Nīlakaṇṭhadīkṣitaviracitaṃ Kaliviḍambanaṃ Sampūrṇam |

*****

Bibiliography

Sincere thanks to all the books refered bring this book.

1.	Kalividambanam	Sri Kamakoti Goshastanam
2.	Kalividambanam	Thanjavur Saraswati Mahal Library
3.	History of classical Sanskrit Literature	Sri M. Krishnamachariar
4.	Shiva Leelarnavam	Sri V Swaminatha Athreya

*****

About the Author

(http://Ramamurthy.jaagruti.co.in)

Dr. Ramamurthy is a versatile personality having experience and expertise in various areas of banking, related IT solutions, information security, IT audit, Vedas, Samskrutam and so on.

His thirst for continuous learning does not subside. Even at the age of late fifties, he did research on a unique topic "Information Technology and Samskrutam" and obtained Ph.D. – doctorate degree from University of Madras. He is into a project of developing a Samskrutam based compiler.

It is his passion to spread his knowledge and experience through conducting classes, training programs and writing books.

He has already published books as detailed below. Further books are in pipe-line.

#	Title	Remarks	Pages
		Indology Related	
1.	*Shrī Lalitā Sahasranāmam*	English Translation of Shrī *Bhāskararāya's Bhāṣyam*	750
2.	Power of *Shrī Vidyā*	The Secrets Demystified – With Lucid English Rendering and Commentaries	80
3.	ஸ்ரீ வித்தையின் ஶக்தி	ஸ்ரீ வித்யா ரகசியங்கள்	100
4.	*Samatā –* समता	An Exposition of Similarities in *Lalitā Sahasranāma* with *Soundaryalaharī, Saptaśatī, Viṣṇu Sahasranāma* and *Shrīmad Bhagavad Gīta*	172
5.	ஸமதா – समता	ஸ்ரீ லலிதா ஸஹஸ்ரநாமம் ஸௌந்தர்யலஹரீ, ஸப்தஶதீ, ஸ்ரீ விஷ்ணு ஸஹஸ்ரநாமம் மற்றும் ஸ்ரீமத் பகவத் கீதைகளில் ஒற்றுமையின் ஒரு வெளிப்பாடு	266
6.	*Advaita* In *Shākta*	Advaita Philosophy Discussed in Shakta Related Books	80
7.	*Shrī Lalitā Triśatī*	300 Divine Names of The Celestial Mother – **English** Translation of *Shrī Ādhi Śaṅkara's Bhāṣyam*	193
8.	ஸ்ரீ லலிதா த்ரிஶதி	300 Divine Names of The Celestial Mother – Tamil Translation of *Shrī Ādi Śaṅkara's Bhāṣyam*	234

#	Title	Remarks	Pages
9.	Secrets of *Mahāśakti*	Chandi Demystified	78
10.	*Daśa Mahā Vidyā*	Ten Cosmic Forms of The Divine Mother	60
11.	ஶ்ரீ வித்யா பேதங்கள்	ஶ்ரீவித்யா உபாசனையின் படிகள் - கோவை ஶ்ரீ சண்டி மலர்	51
12.	*Shrīvidya* Variances	Variances In Srividya Upasana	50
13.	ஶ்ரீ தேவீ ஸ்துதிகள்	பல முக்கிய அம்பாள் ஸ்தோத்ரங்கள்	133
14.	Śrī Devī Stutis – श्रीदेवी स्तुति:	Various Important Stotras of Sri Devi	223
15.	ஷண்மத மந்த்ரங்கள்	பொள்ளாச்சி ஶ்ரீ ஸஹஸ்ரசண்டி மஹாயாக நினைவு மலர்	145
16.	*Śanmata Mantras* – षण्मत मन्त्रा:	Important Mantras Relating to Gods of Six Religions	87
17.	தேவதா மந்த்ரங்கள்	அக்கரைப்பட்டி ஸஹஸ்ரசண்டி மஹாயாக நினைவு மலர்	32
18.	ஆதி ஶங்கரரும் ஷண்மதமும்	ஷண்மதங்களைப் பற்றிய ஒரு அறிமுகம்	32
19.	ஶ்ரீ ஷண்மத தேவதா அர்ச்சனை	ஶ்ரீ மஹா கும்பாபிஷேக மலர்	64
20.	*Vaidhīka* Wedding	Typical Wedding Process in English	56
21.	வைதீகத் திருமணம்	Typical Wedding Process in Tamil	57
22.	ஶ்ரீகுரு பாத பூஜா விதானம்	சித்தகிரி ஸஹஸ்ரசண்டி மலர்	44
23.	குரு வார வழிபாடு		70
24.	ஶ்ரீவித்யா ஶடாம்னாய மந்த்ரங்கள்	சித்தகிரி ஸஹஸ்ரசண்டி மலர்	60
25.	*Ekatā*	Oneness Among Shiva, *Viṣṇu* and Shakti	277
26.	ஏகதா - एकता	ஶிவபெருமான், விஷ்ணு மற்றும் ஶக்திக்குள் ஒற்றுமை	370
27.	*Vedas* – An Analytical Perspective	A Description of Veda, Vedanta, Vedanga, Jyotisha, Shastra, Etc.	240
28.	வேதங்கள் - ஒரு பகுப்பாய்வு	A Description of Veda, Vedanta, Vedanga, Jyotisha, Shastra, Etc.	280
29.	பரமாச்சார்யாள் நோக்கில் ஶ்ரீ லலிதாம்பிகா	The Explanation Given by Paramacharya on Some of The Names in Lalitā Sahasranama	175
30.	*Ṣaṇṇavati Tarpaṇa*	Repaying Debts to Ancestors	42
31.	ஷண்ணவதி தர்பணம்	முன்னோர் கடன் தீர்த்தல்	48
32.	*Shrī Mahā Pratyangirā Devī*	Holy Divine Mother in Ferocious Form	41
33.	ஶ்ரீ மஹா ப்ரத்யங்கிரா தேவீ	தெய்வீக அன்னையின் பயங்கர வடிவம்	51
34.	*Śrī Chakra Navāvarṇam*	Marvels of *Śrī Chakra*	115
35.	ஶ்ரீ சக்ர நவோவர்ணம்	ஶ்ரீ சக்ரத்தின் அதிசயங்கள்	130

#	Title	Remarks	Pages
65.	*Śrī Bhuvaneshwari Devī*	4th Devi of Dasha Maha Vidya	137
66.	ஸ்ரீ புவனேஸ்வரீ தேவீ	4th Devi of Dasha Maha Vidya	151
67.	*Śrī Tripura Bhairavi Devī*	5th Devi of Dasha Maha Vidya	132
68.	ஸ்ரீ த்ரிபுர பைரவீதேவீ	5th Devi of Dasha Maha Vidya	146
69.	*Śrī Kamalātmikā Devī*	6th Devi of Dasha Maha Vidya	138
70.	ஸ்ரீ சின்ன மஸ்தா தேவீ	6th Devi of Dasha Maha Vidya	164
71.	*Śrī Dhūmāvatī Devī*	7th Devi of Dasha Maha Vidya	141
72.	ஸ்ரீ தூ⁴மாவதீ தேவீ	7th Devi of Dasha Maha Vidya	166
73.	*Śrī Bhagalāmukhī Devī*	8th Devi of Dasha Maha Vidya	158
74.	ஸ்ரீ ப³க³லாமுகீ² தேவீ	8th Devi of Dasha Maha Vidya	186
75.	*Śrī Mātangī Devī*	9th Devi of Dasha Maha Vidya	145
76.	ஸ்ரீ மாதங்கீ³ தே³வீ	9th Devi of Dasha Maha Vidya	171
77.	*Śrī Kamalātmikā Devī*	10th Devi of Dasha Maha Vidya	170
78.	ஸ்ரீ கமலாத்மிகா தே³வீ	10th Devi of Dasha Maha Vidya	226
79.	*Chaṇḍī Homa Vidhānam*	Process of Performing Chandi Homam	60
80.	சண்டி ஹோம விதானம்	Process of Performing Chandi Homam	80
81.	ஸ்ரீ ருத்³ர ந்யாசம் & த்ரிஶதீ	300 Divine names of Lord Rudra and Japa Nyasam	224
82.	*Śrī Rudra Nyāsa & Triśatī*	300 Divine names of Lord Rudra and Japa Nyasam	160
83.	ஸ்ரீ ஸூர்ய ஸஹஸ்ர நாமம்	கருத்துக்களுடன் ஒரு விளக்கம்	404
84.	*Śrī Sūrya Sahasranāmam*	Explanation with Comments	320
85.	Kaliviḍambanam	An explanation	75
86.	கலிவிட³ம்ப³னம்	ஒரு விளக்கம்	91
Applied Samskrutam Based			
87.	*Paribhāshā Stora–S*	An Exploration of *Lalitā Sahasranāmam*	96
88.	பரிபாஷா ஸ்தோத்ரங்கள்	ஸ்ரீ லலிதா ஸஹஸ்ரநாமம் - ஒரு ஆய்வு	135
89.	*Shrī Cakra*, An Esoteric Approach	Mathematical Construction to Draw *Shrī Cakra*	64
90.	ஸ்ரீ சக்கரம் வரையும் முறை	ஸ்ரீ சக்கரம் வரைய கணித கட்டுமானம்	84
91.	Number System in Samskrutam	An Overview of Mathematics Based on Samskrutam	123
92.	ஸமஸ்க்ருதத்தில் எண்ணியல்	ஸமஸ்க்ருதத்தில் பொதிந்துள்ள எண் கணிதம்	140
93.	*Vedic* Mathematics	30 Formulae Elucidated	146
94.	Vedic IT	Information Technology and Samskrutam	162
IT Based			
95.	Orthogonal Array	A Statistical Tool for Software Testing	180

#	Title	Remarks	Pages
		Banking Based	
96.	Retail Banking	A Guide Book for Novice	213
97.	Corporate Banking	A Guide Book for Novice	232
98.	Dictionary of Financial Terms	A Guide Book for All – Demystifying Myriad Global Financial Terms	215
99.	GRC In BFS Industry	(**G**overnance, **R**isk Management and **C**ompliance by Banking & Finance Industry)	200

*****

9 789334 195682